LIVING IN THE QUESTION

LIVING IN THE QUESTION

———————

MEDITATIONS

IN THE STYLE OF LECTIO DIVINA

M. BASIL PENNINGTON, O.C.S.O.

Continuum • New York

*This volume
is dedicated to
my friend
Helen
who dared to
live in the question
of Christ's forgiveness
and
now lives
in the wonder of
God's response.*

1999

The Continuum Publishing Company
370 Lexington Avenue, New York, NY 10017

Printed in the United States of America

Library of Congress Cataloging–in–Publication Data

Pennington, M. Basil.
    Living in the question / M. Basil Pennington.
        p.   cm.
    Includes bibliographical references (p.   ).
    ISBN 0-8264-1206-8
    1. Jesus Christ—Teachings Miscellanea. 2. Christian
life—Biblical teaching Miscellanea.   I. Title.
BS2417.C5P46   1999
248.4—dc21   99-34434
                                                CIP

CONTENTS

Be patient toward all that is unsolved in your heart and try to love the questions themselves. Do not seek the answers that cannot be given you, because you would not be able to live them—and the point is to live everything. Live the questions now. Perhaps you will gradually, without noticing it, live along some distant day into the answer.

Rilke

Each one who is born comes into the world as a question for which old answers are not sufficient.

Thomas Merton

WELCOME

Welcome! Would you like to walk with me for a bit—across the pages of life—my life and your life. We will meet the God-Man from Nazareth. He will ask us some questions. Perhaps he will even teach us how to live in the Question.

One of the challenges of my life was a book of answers. And I have gotten into trouble for saying that some of the best heresies that I know are in that book, the Baltimore Catechism. Well, maybe they are not really heresies, but in some ways they are more pernicious.

One of the questions found there is: How did God make me? And the answer: God made me out of nothing. Isn't that a horrible thing to tell a child! If you are made out of nothing, what are you worth? No, God did not make us out of nothing. And he did not make us out of something. But at every moment God brings us forth in his creative love, sharing with us something of his own divine being, goodness and life. That is how much we are loved. We are loved into being.

Another question: Why did God make me? The answer: God made me to know, love and serve him in this world and to be happy with him in the next. That answer has probably driven more out of the Church than any other. Pie in the sky! Serve here, yes, serve. And someday you will find happiness in the next life. Even as a second-grader I could not figure out how I could love God here and not find joy in him. No, this pie-in-the-sky god is not our God. Our God wants us to be happy with him even now, happy in love with him.

Perhaps the most pernicious thing about this catechism though was the pat answers. We had the answers! Well, it didn't take us all that long to grow out of those pat answers. And, having been given the impression that that was the only answer the Church had to offer, we went looking elsewhere for more adequate and satisfying answers.

We don't have all the answers. We do, thank God, have some answers. But answers that give birth to far many more questions. One of the great break-throughs for Thomas Merton on his journey into true freedom was to find the Catholic faith. With that he had something solid on which to stand and from there he went on to face the questions of life. The Church does give some solid answers. There is a God, a God who loves us, loves us so much that he sent his Son to us. And that Son loves us so much that he was willing to die for us. We do have the Eucharist, the other sacraments, the priesthood, the Sacred Scriptures, the living Tradition. When you get down to it, there is not an awful lot that is *de fide,* to be believed on faith, but there is enough to give us something very solid on which to ground our lives.

But there are questions, lots of questions. And it is good to live in the question. A pat answer is closed, it is finished; that's it. It goes no where and leaves little room for hope. A question, the mystery, opens the space for us. It is full of possibility. It gives hope of life and ever more abundant life. Our faith, solid as it might be, is full of questions. And therefore full of life and hope.

Many of us have had the experience of living with a health question. Something has happened, perhaps we have discovered a "lump." The doctor's appointment is a week away. We live with the question. I recently had the experience. It arose early in Holy Week. The doctor's appointment was for Easter Thursday. It added a dimension to this already powerful week for which I was very grateful.

It is paradoxical how much living in a question can bring clarity to our present experience. We see everything in a new perspective. We plum the meaning of each thing more deeply. Each relationship takes on more meaning. We look at each of the loved ones around us and sense the preciousness of our relationship with them, how precious and beautiful they are, even with all their faults, all those little things that so annoy us. The elements of our daily routine have more meaning, we enjoy them with a sense of their wholesomeness: our exercise program, our morning shower, the consoling words of Scripture, the quiet, strengthening moments of resting in the Lord in prayer, meals, work. Whatever the outcome, we know there is this bedrock we can stand on. Living in the question, even with all its fears—and these are very real, even if we do manage to reign in our imagination and not let it run away with us—is a grace, giving a time of heightened realization, a fuller, more vital time of life.

But we do not need to wait until we are hit by something like this sort of medical question to begin to live in the question and let it give a certain vitality to our daily life. We can each day choose one of the ultimate questions of our lives and let it be really with us. It doesn't have to be bad news or what we are inclined to sense as bad news: What if I am to die tonight? What if I lose my sight? Hearing? Ability to walk? (Living with such questions can certainly give us a heightened appreciation for these gifts we take so for granted and an increased joy in our everyday use of them.) It can be a question of something very good: What if I meet someone today who becomes a true friend with whom I can share *everything?* What if today I have a real experience of God and his intense personal love for me? What if today I get a new job offer? Or win the lottery? We can choose any real question and live with it for a bit, letting it cast its light on our daily routine and we find it does make a difference, a very enriching difference.

A possibility I would like to suggest is this: live with the questions the Lord Jesus asks. Take up a Bible and open to the Gospels. Look for the questions Jesus asks of us: Who do you say that I am? What do you want? Are you not worth more than many sparrows? Why do you not believe? Living with these, one after the other—and there are many in the Gospels—can bring us to a wholly other, much richer perspective on our lives, maybe to seeing our lives the way God sees them, shot through with the light, the joy, the fullness of a risen life of Christ.

We need to uncover within ourselves the mechanisms of ideology—whether it be universalism or spiritualism or any other—and root them out. It isn't just a matter of changing the answers we carry around with us that profoundly influence our way of acting and the way we relate with others. We need to change the very questions from which such answers flow. Listening open-minded to the questions of Jesus can help us do this. We are halfway there and more when we begin to ask the right questions. Jesus asks the right questions.

We hear his questions. They are asked in us in the context of our own particular perspective. We have to go deeper and let them question even that perspective. The questions of Jesus are articulations of the questions that arise out of our own true self; questions which, in accepting the false self as completely as we have, we have succeeded in totally muting. If we dare to let Jesus' questions truly resound within us we will discover that they are already there as the questions our own deepest self asks us.

This is precisely the work of true, living theology: *fides quaerens intellectum,* faith seeking understanding. The questions of Jesus which come to us through his revealing word, call us to open to a new understanding of God, of ourselves, of our sisters and brothers, of the creation and its purpose. What does God's revelation in Christ Jesus mean right now as we struggle for liberation not only for ourselves and within ourselves from our passions, prejudices and blindness but for all our fellows, the poor, the Black, the woman, the man, the disabled, the homosexual . . . ? The questions of Jesus have to be heard in their historical context: not only that of the past—the work of biblical exegesis—but also that of the present— the work of theology using the biblical exegesis but also all the stuff of life. As Juan Luis Segundo said: "God shows up in a different light when his people find themselves in different historical settings." And this work of theology does not belong only to the professional theologians. It is the task of every rational person gifted with faith, recipient of the revelation. It is your task and mine.

Don't let this word "theology" scare you. I don't mean the academic quasi-science, though I don't exclude it. I mean rather the ordinary everyday task of the faithful person trying to make sense out of her or his life in the light of what has been learned from the Lord—letting God be part of the dialogue—in discerning how to live today as a descent, contributing, human person. This involves not only horizontal relationships but a vertical relationship that grounds and balances.

Is it the same God who in the Psalms is wrathful toward his enemies and who calls upon the sons of Abraham to annihilate the people of Canaan and then tells us in the New Testament to turn the other cheek; who in New Testament times tells slaves to obey their masters and today in his Church proclaims that equal dignity and freedom are due to all human persons? I can't say: obviously it is. It is not obvious to many. I believe it is and perhaps too readily I fall back on his word in Isaiah: My thoughts are not your thoughts nor my ways your ways but as high as the heavens are above the earth so are my thoughts beyond your thoughts and my ways beyond your ways. I need to live in the question. What is one to say today to people who are in a situation akin to that of the ancient Israelites? I recently spent some weeks in East Africa and I came to ask myself: are there unforgivable sins? Can, should a woman who has been savagely raped and has seen her husband, children and parents hacked to death with machetes, turn the other cheek and simply forgive?

It is not always comfortable to live in the question. In fact, it usually isn't. What makes it attractive is the potential it gives us for rising to a newer richer life. But we like our comfort. We are prone to choose present comfort over future gain. Indeed, how many of us fill our lives with doing to avoid the quiet moments when the questions might arise. We are made in the very image of God, so we are mystery. We are question, infinite question. We can avoid living in the question only by avoiding our true self, devoting ourselves to building up a false self made up of what I do, what I have, what others think of me. We want to have "the answer"—the answer that will answer all, so that we can have everything under control, so that we can sense the power.

God is the answer. And God is mystery, God is the question.

If we are really honest with ourselves and let the questions of life, the questions of Christ truly question us, they have the potency to change our lives. And through our lives, change the world. In the first days of our Cistercian Order there arrived at the gates of the New Monastery, the Abbey of Citeaux, a rather delicate young man, Bernard of Fontaines. He was twenty-two. Up to that time he had lived a rather scholarly and pious life, unfamiliar with the rigors of knightly life or the labors of the surf. Soon he found himself in the fields with the other novices, bent over in the very hard work of harvesting. He quickly fell behind the others, totally exhausted. Such an experience could have led to depression, despair, abandonment of his vocation. But Bernard took refuge in a question. He kept asking himself: *Bernarde, ut quid venisti?* Bernard, why have you come? I don't know what answers he came up with on a day to day basis during those cruel novitiate days. But in fact his whole life was the answer. Within a couple years he was Bernard, Abbot of Clairvaux, the spiritual father, the leader, the most powerful figure of his century. His commentary on the love song of Solomon, the crowning gem of a rich literary heritage, is his exquisitely beautiful but nonetheless stammering attempt to answer the question. It is a question that strikes deep at the root of life—all our lives: For what have you come?

When Jesus asks a question he is sometimes taking the initiative; other times, like the good rabbi that he is, he is responding to a question with a question. This leaves the openness, the space for growth, for life, for everything. But then maybe, too, the Lord is saying there is no

answer. Because, in fact, there is no question. Love has no
questions. It is the ground of all, accepts all. There are
questions only where there is division, absence, estrange-
ment, alienation from the ground of being, which is God.

Nonetheless, Jesus does question. And sometimes
his are true questions. More often they are questions to
get us to question, to open the space within us to receive
his teaching. And the questions themselves are a teaching. Thomas Merton has said that a person is best known
by the questions he asks. As we listen to the questions
of Jesus we come to know what is important to him, his
respect for others, his compassion and deep human understanding, and many other things. Listen to the questions
of Jesus and before you begin to ask yourself the question
and formulate an answer, ask: What does this question
tell me about the Questioner? Indeed, if I am answering
him, it is the context within which I want to frame my
answer. When I go on to ask the question of myself, I
find another very different context. This is just one of
the many reasons why the same question can have so
many different answers. I ask the question and give my
answers in the light of the reality I am living in: the
boredom, the loneliness, the anxiety, the suffering, the
death, the terror, the oppression, the joy, the love. I hear
the questions and formulate my answers in the context
of dialogue, with the Lord, with Jesus. Together we talk
and wonder about profound questions. We look at them
one way and then another. We accept the ambiguities.
We are willing to leave things unanswered or partially
answered—for now. It is all in context. We are together
today, so the questions are different, the answers are different. The big issues come to play: nuclear potential,
wars and armament, ecological danger, marginality,

oppression and the oppressed, the displaced, the victims of all sort of injustices. We identify with each; separateness is only a dream. We are one humanity called to enter into one divinity in this questioning Jesus who helps us sort out the answers.

As we listen to the questions of Jesus we want also to be aware of who is being asked. This is also certainly part of the context. And we might move from there and repeat the question, asking it now of others in the group present to Jesus at the time and to others in other times and places, never failing at some point to ask it of ourselves. I might ask myself also, is this question Jesus asks my question. Is it a real question for me in my life on my journey?

We all have our questions, some more, some less, some more profound, more disturbing, more challenging, more frightening to ourselves, to the upholders of Orthodoxy. Do they all fit within the questions of Jesus? A good question.

As we answer Jesus' question we do not want to fail to listen to the answer that was given to him on the occasion when he first asked it—and how he responded to the answer he was given. This will undoubtedly lead us forward in our own response. And what other responses does revelation, the sacred Scriptures offer to this particular question? Jesus was speaking to a people who lived and thought in a biblical context. The whole of the Hebrew Bible as well the whole revelation of his own life is the context within which he frames his question and within which his hearers hear it.

At the same time, I hear the question within the context of my own life. And I need to respond in that same context. That was part of the problem of the catechism. It not only gave me the questions, some very important questions, but it also gave me the answers, set answers, which were supposed to do for everyone. And, sad to say, often never really touched the life of anyone and became a living answer out of which one began to live. Each one of us is an absolutely unique expression of God, of God's love, of the Love that God is. And each of us therefore has an absolutely unique relationship with God. If I am going to find the true answers for me now, for the Christ-person that I am, I must leave behind all my preconceived ideas and the preconceived ideas of others. And let the truth emerge from the here and now reality of this word of God rising within me. "I live, now not I, but Christ lives within me." It is with a strong faith in that reality that I am capable of living now in uncertainty, mystery and even doubt without reaching out irritably for some fact or reason to hang on to. Yes, I am one with Christ, one with all others in Christ, but I am a unique. Yes, I am one of the People of God, I live intimately in community, yet I am an absolutely unique person. And the Lord's question to me is not, why are you not like Saint Bernard or Saint Basil or any other saint. His question to me is: why are you not Basil. His questions to us have really one aim: to murder the false self (The Lord is quite graphic when he talks about his reaction to this our false self: I feel like vomiting you out of my mouth.) and thus open the space for the emergence of our true self.

When President Clinton visited Moscow in 1998, the Russians had a bit of fun at his expense. You probably have seen those Russian dolls made of wood, rather rotund little things, with the face and clothes painted on them. When you unscrew the top of the first you find a second doll inside of the same style and shape but painted with another figure. This second one in turn opens to give forth a third, and so on. A favorite for the Russians was a doll of the Czar which opened to reveal the Czarinna, who in turn gave forth the oldest princess, and on down the line. For the more pious there was the doll of Christ which opened to reveal the Blessed Mother and then in turn the favorite saints of Russia. When the American President arrived in Moscow, Clinton dolls were much in evidence on Red Square. I think you can probably guess who was found inside them.

Scripture is a bit like a Russian doll. After we have carefully examined and enjoyed the surface, the literal and historical meaning, we need to open it and let it reveal to us its hidden meanings. Saint Paul, under the inspiration of Holy Spirit, set the tone for this. He would speak of a passage from the Hebrew Bible, like Abraham's two wives. Then he would say: "This is an allegory" and he would open out a deeper meaning: These two wives stand for the two covenants.

The Fathers took this up and began to explore several "spiritual" senses: the allegorical, the moral and the ana-gogical or unitive. Like so many smaller dolls they were to be found within the literal sense. This rich exploration of Scripture reached its peak with the great Cistercian Fathers of the twelfth century just as the more scholastic and rational way of theologizing was beginning to take over in the Church. It isn't connatural for us to follow this kind of exegesis. We have to make some effort after we have explored a text quite fully to unscrew it and let yet another meaning with all its potential to emerge. Not so long ago scripture scholars were speaking a good bit about the *sensus plenior,* the fuller sense or meaning of scriptural texts. There is an excess of meaning in God's word, whether it be the first word of Creation, the Eternal Word or the word of revelation. Our sharp logical categories are just not adequate. Nor our dualistic antinomies, a purely dialectic methodology of either/or. The reality is both/and: both life and death, eternity and history, myth and fact, revelation and reason, spiritual and empirical, unity and duality and even trinity, dialectic and analogy, stability and adaptability, truth and indeterminacy.

We, sons and daughters of a more rational age, are not readily comfortable with the logic of Fathers, a logic that does not progress: major, minor and conclusion, one point after another. Rather one thought, one image, the color of one word leads off to another. Aelred of Reivaulx in a Palm Sunday sermon will let the cord that bound the donkey lead him to speak of Samson who was bound by a sevenfold cord. On Christmas, the shepherds exclamation: Let us go over and see, opens the way for Aelred to speak of Moses who said of the burning bush: Let us go over and see.

But isn't this the way it usually happens when we are sitting with a friend in conversation? One idea leads to another, one thought gives birth to another, image after image evokes memories and facts. We don't usually worry too much about the logical sequence of our conversation and sharing. But it is so satisfying because it doesn't stay in the head, it calls forth imagination, memory and emotion and lodges in the heart.

As we enter the world of the Gospels we need to let our imagination have full play. Jesus was a story teller. Someday just for fun sit down and make a list of all the different images Jesus uses as he brings to us the great revelation: shepherd, prodigal father, unjust judge, poor widow, fisherman, sewer, vine, seed, well, winnowing fan, wineskin, new wine and old, hidden treasure, a pearl of great price, and on and on and on. With stories and images Jesus sews his message in our minds and hearts.

It is true. For us today, for some of us, not all Jesus' stories work. Our sisters and brothers in Alaska are not readily touched by the image of a sewer or even of a shepherd. Nor is an inner city lad in New York who has never gotten out of the city. True, today TV and Internet make these images more real for the snowbound or city-bound, but the image of shepherd will never speak to them like it does to the boy in the pastures of Palestine or even in the Rockies or the New Zealand hills. With imagination we can legitimately and effectively transform these stories. The Eskimo will get the feel of a story about his sleigh dogs. The New Yorker could be encouraged to plant some radishes in a tin can but more readily will he feel a story about a good cop or counsellor or a good priest, a Father Flanagan or a Father Bruce Ritter. We do have to admit that women do not feature very often in Jesus' stories, though they certainly are very present in the Jesus story. His stories, given the audience he was usually addressing, were about men doing men's things. There certainly is room here for transposition.

There used to be a very pious archbishop who regularly came to our monastery on retreat. While with us he would preside at the Sunday liturgy and give a homily. His style never varied. He would begin: I have three points for you. . . . He would then enumerate the three points and then develop them. Finally he would conclude: Now I have given you three points . . . and he would again set them forth. I have never forgotten his style but for the life of me I can't remember a single point he gave us. But who will ever forget it, once he has heard the story of the good shepherd, of the prodigal father, of

Jesus washing Peter's feet? The whole life of Jesus is a revelation story.

Images, more than thoughts, evoke feelings within us, all sorts of emotions. These too we want to listen to. They impact a great deal on how we respond. And more important, how we respond in our lives to the ideas that the revelation evokes in our minds. We all know the experience that Saint Paul so candidly shares with us: the good I know I do not do and the evil I abhor I do do. A lot of this is due to the fact that we know the good only in our minds but the strong attractive pleasure of the evil we know emotionally and visually in our imaginations and memories. This is another reason why stories can be so much more effective than ideas to make a difference in our lives. With the stories come images and they evoke emotions, memories and feelings that speak more directly and powerfully to the heart. It is experience, even this kind of inner imaginative experience, that moves us far more than abstract concepts, no matter how lofty and good. New ideas calling for conversion have a hard time making any headway against a flood of stored up memories rich in feeling. There are, thanks be to God, the powerful touches of grace that do enable us to make some headway. But if we school ourselves to use our imaginations and feelings as we fill our storehouse with the good news of the revelation, it will be able to have more impact on our lives and more easily bring us into joy and peace.

I had originally thought of writing a book on the answers of Jesus to see if they answered my questions today. Well, I found Jesus asked more questions than gave answers. He was a good rabbi. And what answers he does give are full of space for many more questions to arise. Even our carefully formulated dogmas, which some people seeking security latch on to, if you really think about them, yield more questions than air-tight answers. We tried hard in our polemic to define just who was a member of the Church. We carefully developed Saint Paul's image of the body—that's a fairly clear image. But we found it just didn't work. So we are now back to the age-old image of the People, a motley crew, and it is never all that clear who is in and who is out. And in truth the Second Vatican Council came around to saying that in one way or another everybody is in; just how much in, that is up to each one of us with our respective grace and freedom. David Tracey said so well: "Real religion does not give final answers; it makes us ask better questions." Living inside the right questions makes the difference.

In the pages that follow we confront, or rather let confront us, only a very few of the questions that Jesus expressly asks in the course of those inspired written records of his earthly life which we call the Gospels. In an appendix I have listed others so that you may continue on your own or, better, with others in faith sharing. If you ever exhaust this list there are an inexhaustible number of implicit questions. There is even the inexhaustible question of God himself, the mystery of love that will ever call us forth, revealing to us more and more the depth of our own mystery—a mystery of unfathomable beauty and goodness, image of his own.

I have frequently been asked what English-language translation of the Bible I like best. I actually prefer the *Jerusalem Bible*. I think Father Alexander did a good job in producing a Bible that is beautifully written and yet still very faithful to the text as it was known at the time of his work. It has been surpassed by the *New Jerusalem Bible* which benefits from later scholarship but unfortunately does not retain all the beauty of the earlier translation. In this volume I use my own translations from the Greek which aim at literalness more than style, hoping to let the original words speak more directly to us.

I have put a lot of myself into these pages. In recent years many have asked me to write an autobiography. I do not have the courage for such an undertaking. But I am happy to share myself, especially in the context of the Gospels for that is the context within which I seek to live. It is our privilege as Christians, disciples and friends of Jesus.

One of the most powerful books in all literature, almost lost in the Bible, is the Book of Job. Powerful because it confronts one of the most agonized of all human questions: the sufferings of the just. After hours and hours of "wise" efforts on the part of his friends to come up with a satisfying answer, a rather exasperated God finally speaks up: "Who is this that obscures divine plans with words of ignorance?" And he confronts poor, long-suffering Job: "Gird yourself and stand up like a man. I will question you and you tell me the answers." And the Lord takes off in a litany of questions that every scientist should ask himself before setting forth his wise findings. "Where were you when I founded the earth? . . . Who determined its size? . . . Have you ever in your lifetime commanded the morning and shown the dawn its place? . . . Do you give the horse his strength? . . . Is it by your discernment that the hawk soars?" On and on the questions go in a magnificent poetical array. Job's answer in the end: "I know you can do all things . . . things too wonderful for me which I cannot know." In the end we do not have the answers. Rather we have the grace and the joy of entering ever more deeply, confidently and peacefully into the great Question, who is our God, the God of mystery, the God of love—into the Mystery of Love.

M. BASIL PENNINGTON, O.C.S.O.

The Feast of the Incarnation, 1998
St. Joseph's Abbey, Spencer, MA

1

WHAT DO YOU WANT?

> As John stood there with two of his disciples, he saw
> Jesus walking by and he said: Look, the Lamb of God.
> Hearing this, the two disciples followed Jesus. Jesus
> turned around and saw them following and said to
> them: What do you want?
>
> —John 1:35–38

History has a way of repeating itself, again and again. In our own time we have seen many young, and not so young, go off to the East in search of some wisdom, some deeper answers, some way to make more sense out of life. This quest has been a reoccurring human experience. In the fourth century my own patron, Saint Basil, with his friend Saint Gregory, left the study halls of Athens and headed east in search of a fuller wisdom. Not long after a young Dalmatian, John Cassian by name, did the same, leaving the schools of Rome. These were among many, including women: Paula the Younger and her grandmother, Paula the Elder, Macrina, the sister of Saint Basil, and so many others.

A few centuries earlier, a couple of young fishermen, laboring on the banks of the Sea of Galilee, experienced the same deep questioning and felt the same yearning to look for a wise master who could show them the way and give them some of the answers to life. John and Andrew heard the gossip that was racing about. There had recently emerged from the desert to the east of Jordan, the river into which their own lake flowed, a strange prophetic figure. He had lived long in the desert. He wore a rough smock made of camel's hair. He ate only the wild food that one might find in the wilderness: honey and locusts. And he had a stirring message. Many were flocking to him. Because he was "baptizing" them in the waters of the Jordan, putting them through a ritual of purification, he was now called John the Baptizer. The two young fishermen wondered if this man might not be the great prophet foretold by Moses. If so, he would surely have some answers. Even if he wasn't the great prophet, he might still have something to say, something worth hearing. Soon, the two left their fellow workers and their families and headed east.

It was an exciting and excited throng that they joined when they reached the other side of the Jordan. The man from the desert certainly was a prophet and had a message. But was he the one? This question was put to him and, with an impressive humility, John replied very straightforwardly. No, he was not the one, the great prophet. He was rather the forerunner. The prophet was to come, and come soon. Now was the time of preparation, the time for repentance and purification in preparation for the great prophet's coming.

John the Fisherman and Andrew stayed with the throng that surrounded John. They became his disciples—for the time being, waiting eagerly for the coming of the other one.

One day, as the Baptizer was preaching, he suddenly became transfixed. His eyes shone. He raised his hand and pointed, out beyond the crowd. "Look! There is the Lamb of God!" Andrew and John heard. And they wasted no time.

They were off—seeking to catch up with the Lamb of God.

As they approached, Jesus turned. He saw the eager young faces, the glistening eyes. And Jesus addressed to them the question he constantly addresses to each one of us: "What do you want?" Jesus will give us whatever we want. He has said, "Ask and you shall receive."

Young John, moved undoubtedly by the same Spirit who had stirred his inner being in the first place and had sent him on his search, was in touch with the deepest longings of his being. Moreover, this man who looked upon him now, this "Lamb of God," evoked in him a strange and wondrous feeling, one that can only be called love. John knew what he wanted. It was not any particular thing. All too often our response to Jesus' open and wholehearted generosity is a request for some puny, passing, partial thing, some bauble that seems at the moment to be the key to happiness, but which always leaves us in the end unsatisfied. Even the loftiest of God's gifts is not enough. The great King Solomon, when asked by the Lord, "What do you want?" asked for wisdom. He was highly commended by the Lord for such a lofty choice. But it was not enough. In the end, his heart, unsatisfied, went astray.

We will never find this beloved disciple asking, like the impetuous Peter: Lord, we have left everything for you; what are we going to get? Little enough did Peter leave—a leaky boat and some worn nets. But he got a good deal from the Lord: a hundredfold in this life and life eternal. And yet, all that would not be enough for a lover like John, if it did not include living with the One he loved.

As Saint Augustine has said, "Our hearts are made for you, O Lord, and they will not rest until they rest in you." The young fishermen from Galilee's shores somehow knew this. Their answer to the Lord's openness: Where do you live? Where do you dwell. They wanted no particular thing from him. They wanted him himself. They wanted to move right in with him.

They wanted all. And in the end they got it. John would forever speak of himself as "the disciple whom Jesus loved."

"Where do you live?" "Come and see," was Jesus' reply. And they followed him. It was not a short journey. In fact, it lasted years. And they learned that, unlike the foxes who had their dens and the birds of the air who had their nests, the Son of Man had not whereon to lay his head. But they finally did get their answer. It was at that very special meal we have come to refer to as the "Last Supper."

The two from the Lake had been joined by others, including their own blood brothers. And all these disciples were constantly asking their questions, rather stupid, uncomprehending questions often enough. So it was on that special night. One after the other, they made fools of themselves, fighting for precedence, not comprehending Jesus' powerful ritual acts, nor his words that were freighted with meaning beyond their present unaided comprehension.

It came Judas' turn to ask. "Lord, what is this all about?"

Jesus replied, and in so doing, he finally gave the answer to John and Andrew's question of old. For the first time since that day of original encounter, the Gospel of John, which carefully records all of these moments, uses again that beautiful Greek expression which might best he translated "make one's home." "Rabbi, where do you live? where do you dwell? where do you make your home?" "I make my home in you."—that is essentially what Jesus said.

"If anyone loves me that one will keep my word, and my Father will love such a one, and we shall come to that one and make our home with that one."

God-Jesus does indeed dwell everywhere. Everywhere is his. And yet, in all of creation there is no place that he more likes to call home than the human heart. We are his favorite dwelling place in all that he has made. This is why he created—and created all there is. To find a home of love within us. As he once told another of his lovers, Theresa of Avila: If I had not made the world, I would make it just for you. So he would speak to each of us, if we would but listen.

It is difficult for most of us to believe such love, to believe as John did. So much has been the negative feedback that has been heaped upon us as we go along life's way. So much has the production orientation of our society penetrated our thinking and our evaluations that we think we are only worth what we do, or what we have, or what others think of us. We do not know how precious we are in ourselves. As Dame Julian of Norwich, that delightful English mystic declared, we are God's dream, his homiest home.

We have too little respect for ourselves, too little esteem for our own importance. God sees things otherwise. He thinks so much of us, he gave his very Son for each of us. And that Son so esteems us, so loves us, that he literally died for us. Greater love than this no one has. . . . As the Second Vatican Council proclaimed in its remarkable pastoral constitution, *Joy and Hope,* we have immeasurable dignity for we are in fact the very image of God himself.

Because we have such a deflated appreciation of our true self we find it difficult to believe that anyone, not to speak of God, could actually love us—love us with a wholly gratuitous love. This is why we cannot hear him asking us: What do you want? Or we can't believe what we hear when these words are addressed to us. Or we fail to take them seriously, when we do hear them. Or, when we do begin to take them seriously, we ask for so little. We dare not ask for too much, for much at all. For All! For the All that we truly want. For who are we?

I personally believe our greatest sin is that we expect too little of ourselves because we expect too little of our God.

Now then:

What do you want?

2

WHAT DID YOU GO OUT TO THE DESERT TO SEE?

> Jesus began to speak to the crowds about John: What
> did you go out to the desert to see? A reed swayed by
> the wind? Then what did you go out to see? Someone
> dressed in fine clothing? Behold, those in fine clothes
> are in the houses of kings. Then why did you go out? To
> see a prophet? Yes, I tell you, and more than a prophet.
> —Matthew 11:7–9

What did you go out to see? A reed swaying in the wind? No! Today, in a world that is indeed swaying and more than swaying, indeed where the social order, the moral order and the economic order are in many respects in chaos, we are desperately seeking something stable, something we can count on. There seems to be nothing we can count on. People's word? When men and women shed their marriage partners without a thought of their marriage vows. Business agreements? When businesses are mercilessly wiped out by hostile take-overs or ambitious connivance. Employment contracts? When down-sizing suddenly puts a person's whole career behind her or him with nothing ahead. The sworn statement, the oath of office? When a president lies and abuses his office. We do not have to go out to the desert to see swaying reeds. We unfortunately can see them everywhere. What we long to see is someone of integrity on whom we can count.

What did you go out to the desert to see? Someone dressed in fine clothing? No! This going out is the journey of those who have come to realize fine clothes, beautiful homes, stylish cars, luxuries of all sorts are not enough for real happiness. We can find all these things easily enough in our affluent society. Even we monks who are supposed to be poor with the poor Christ find ourselves in a beautiful home, are well clothed and fed, have all our needs taken care of and are assured of that for the rest of our lives. But we did not come out to the desert for all this, for we could have had it well enough where we came from, in the midst of our families and loved ones.

Then why did we go out? To see a prophet? Yes! And more. Someone who can point the way. Again and again and again in history, we have gone out. Andrew and John worked with their families on the Sea of Galilee. And these friends said to one another: There has to be more to life than catching fish. And they headed east (It always seems to be east!) across the Jordan where they heard there was a prophet. My own patron, Basil and his friend Gregory were studying in the prestigious schools of Athens, drinking in what wisdom the great lecturers had to offer. And they, too, said: There has to be something more. And they headed east out to the desert in search of the wise Fathers and Mothers who were reported to be there. And many others in their time, women as well as men, followed the same route. I particularly like the couple Melania the Elder and Melania the Younger, a grandmother and her granddaughter. I have always pictured mother at home, wringing her hands: Not only my daughter but my mother, too! In the eleventh century the courageous old abbot of Molesme, Robert by name, led twenty of his monks forth from what was in fact a very prosperous and holy monastery but one becoming more and more immeshed in worldly affairs. He led them into the wastelands and marsh beyond Dijon, a place called Citeaux. And many other monastic founders of that century did likewise. And in our own day the numbers of those who have headed east or into the wilderness or off to the hermitage are beyond any counting.

Those who went out to the desert to see the Baptizer did go to see a prophet. He was a true prophet who pointed to the Truth. He humbly protested: I am not the One. He pointed beyond himself. Yes, a true prophet. And more than a prophet. For he was indeed the very forerunner of the Lord himself.

And the day came. At first it seemed like any other day on Jordan's bank, as John harangued the crowds, gave them his salutary message, and baptized all who wanted to change their lives and prepare for the coming. But then he came: Behold the Lamb of God. The Lamb of sacrifice who was to save and reconcile all. The one Lamb of God, the Lamb who is God, perfect, complete forever. This is what we all truly want: a Saviour who so loves us that he will even lay down his life for us. One who can reconcile us with ourselves, our true selves, bring peace, joy and harmony into our lives. One who can reconcile us with all, with the whole creation, show us how to care for it, love it, give it meaning, the true meaning it has from God its Creator.

This particular story is an Advent Gospel. It is meant to prepare us, point the way, guide us to the fulfilment of our deepest desires. When Andrew and John went out to the desert and the more-than-a-prophet John pointed out the Lamb, they immediately ran after him. As they caught up to him, he turned and in substance asked the very same question he now asks: What are you seeking? What do you want? And this keen young seeker, another John, helps us to uncover the true answer.

Most of us most of the time are all caught up in activities. We are caught up with our possessions, trying to keep up with the Joneses. But no matter how busy we are, there come those moments when something deep within us tells us: this is not enough; this can't be all that there is in life. We really don't want to wait until we are waylaid by such realizations. We all need, at least at times, to take time. Like John we need to ask: Where do you dwell? And go to that place deep within. There we will find our truest self and hear more clearly the yearning of our own heart. That is the desert for most, the desert of their own heart, where the great Prophet dwells, Truth himself.

He has said: ask and you shall receive; seek and you will find. Unfortunately we ask for the ephemeral which isn't really satisfying. We seek what is passing and will leave us empty—until we come to realize in truth we do not know what we truly want, where our true happiness lies. We need to seek a teacher, a prophetic voice—the guidance of one whom the Lord has sent, the Church who makes Jesus present to us today, Jesus who is all that our hearts seek. Until we seek and find the Truth we will in fact be in a desert chasing mirages, encountering delusions, finding all swaying and unstable.

We need to stop, to let go of all the surface stuff, and go into the desert of our heart. And listen. Then knowing our emptiness and deepest longings, we go seek the prophetic wisdom that can point the way. If we do not take time to listen to our deepest longings, if we constantly drown them out with our activities and distractions, we can never hope to find true happiness. Nonetheless we are tempted to do this because we suspect that what the "prophet" is going to ask is not going to be all that easy. But what alternative do we have? Can we keep running all our lives? Keep ourselves ever distracted. Some certainly try, with alcohol, drugs, sex, the boob-tube. What a life! Is it a life? How different is a life that knows it has the Answer: the Way, the Truth and the Life, Eternal Life. We all have to ask ourselves: What am I going to seek? Endless activity? Amassed goods? Or am I going to moderate all this and find some desert spaces and desert places where I can listen to the wisdom of my own heart and encounter—yes, more than a prophet: Divine Truth himself abiding lovingly within my heart, not just pointing but ready to gently and most lovingly lead me along the Way to the fullness of Life.

3

WHAT DO YOU WANT ME TO DO FOR YOU?

And it came to pass that as Jesus drew near Jericho a certain blind man sat by the road begging. And hearing a crowd passing through he asked what this might be. They told him: Jesus the Nazarene is passing by. And he cried out: Jesus, son of David, have pity on me. The people going before Jesus scolded the man telling him he should be quiet. But he kept calling out all the more, Son of David, pity me. And stopping, Jesus commanded that he be brought to him. When he drew near, Jesus asked him: What do you want me to do for you? And the blind man asked that he may see again. And Jesus said to him: See again! Your faith has healed you. The man saw again and he followed Jesus glorifying God.

—Luke 18:35–43

Mark's Gospel tells us the man's name: he was Bartimaeus, the son of Timaeus. As he sat by the side of the road just outside of Jericho he had heard the gossip about the young carpenter—or should we say rabbi from Nazareth. Bartimaeus had come to his own conclusions about the man, maybe fuelled in part by his own hopes and imaginings. Indeed by this time just about everybody had heard about Jesus. And there were a lot of diverse opinions about him. John, his forerunner, sent his own disciples to publicly question Jesus, hoping this might bring forth a clear declaration on the matter. And Jesus was clear enough, appealing to the very evident signs that marked his daily ministry: the blind see, the lame walk, lepers are cleansed, the deaf hear and the dead rise and the poor have good news preached to them. It was clear to anyone who could hear with an open heart: this was the Messiah.

Many in this world hear a cry in the depths of their own heart. And hope that there is a fulfllment—if only it would come. This is why evangelization—even in this age of dialogue and with full respect for peoples' already established religious convictions—continues to be important. And why the proclamation of the Good News is heard: because it is already in the heart of every human person. As the great Augustine put it: Our hearts are made for you. O God. . . . When it is heard it is simply recognized: This is what I have been waiting for, hoping for.

Bartimaeus heard and he believed: This Jesus is the Son of David, the Messiah. It is hard for us Christians and I suspect even for most Jews today to realize what this title meant for a Jew of Jesus' time. The Messiah was an image that brought together all the age-old hopes of a deeply religious people with the aspirations of an enslaved people. It was a powerful statement for this man to cry out: Son of David—shocking for some, maybe many. Perhaps that was why they sought to quiet him. Bartimaeus, as he sat there begging, must have often imagined what he would do if this Jesus came his way. And now the news was told him: He is here! And Bartimaeus was not going to let his chance pass him by.

Yes, they tried to silence him. As we try to cry out to the Lord in faith a lot of "rational" voices, both within and without try to silences us.

We hear that prayer is useless or at least unnecessary, at least prayer of petition. After all, didn't Jesus say that the Father already knows what we need before we ask him. I had a good man here on retreat last week who said precisely that: "I never ask God for anything. It isn't necessary." Apart from the fact that Jesus did say very explicitly: Ask and you shall receive, and even told that very daring story where he likened God to an unjust judge giving way to a pestering old woman, coming to a friend with our needs is of the very fabric of friendship. God did not simply make this world and toss it out there to leave it to go along on its own. Indeed, at every moment the Lord brings his creation forth in creative love. And he has willed that the way he is going to bring forth this world in the next hour, the next day, the next year, the next millennium, depends in part on what we ask of him. Our prayers of petition are very powerful in the providence of God.

But should someone as wretched as me bother God? I recall that day when Jesus came upon another afflicted wretch. And Jesus' disciples, seeking to sort out the theology of the day, asked the Master: Lord, who sinned: this man or his parents? Jesus replied, immediately taking them to a higher plane where true theology is to be found: Neither; this is for the glory of God. The Apostle Paul would later tells us: For those who love God, all things work together unto good. The greatest good: God's glory. We see that here in this event of healing. And our good, too. For in accepting our afflictions and offering them with Jesus' own saving passion we have the glory of sharing with him in the healing and wholing of this world of ours.

The Jews surrounding Jesus for the most part would have been convinced that this man was blind because he was a sinner. But that would be no problem for Jesus. As he told the Pharisees on another occasion, he came for sinners. Sin is never an obstacle to our being heard by the

Lord. In fact it is an admission ticket if we come to him repentant and wanting change.

This poor man belonged to the "unwashed," the street people, the people who lived in the slums. Even today, sad to say, they are not that welcome in our fine churches. Often there are not even little churches for them in their miserable slums. Dioceses are quick to see that fine churches are built in new suburbs but not in the favelas; the inner city churches are the ones that are being closed, big, old structures that have been allowed to deteriorate. Of course, there is a lot of good "rational" reasoning behind this way of acting. And happily things are changing. The People of God are more fully embracing Jesus' option for the poor, though in some places this is more in theory than in fact. Yet we see in many places, given the opportunity, it is these poor unwashed ones, the harijohns in India, the Hakka in Taiwan, the tribals in China, who are most ready to embrace the Good News and celebrate it in their lives.

Are not Blacks often lumped right in with these poor wretches? And people of color in the "white man's church?" And gays and lesbians? They are disordered, messed up. They cannot approach the Son of David unless they are ready to forsake a deep part of themselves, their sexuality, and all hope of intimacy and committed union.

But Bartimaeus kept shouting. Nobody's ideas about respectability were going to deprive him of his hope, keep him from bringing his need to the Lord.

"Bring him to me." What a moment!

Jesus appreciates faith. We can recall the day the Centurion, a pagan, a member of the oppressing army, spoke simply but eloquently of Jesus' authority over disease. Even Jesus was in admiration of such faith. How often had Jesus' word to petitioners been: Your faith has saved you. He looked at this poor blind man. Jesus' reputation had gone before him. And faith comes through hearing. This man may be blind but he could and did hear. Jesus' response to such faith was very direct, a powerful question: What do you want me to do for you? It is a question depending on faith for an answer. We want something from him only because we believe he can give it and wants to. Again, I believe our greatest sin is that we expect too little from ourselves and for ourselves because we expect too little from God. We will not ask because we do not believe he can give it or has the good will, or the good will in regards to us, to give it. Jesus shows his good will here and throughout the Gospels. We have but to listen with open ear and heart and with Bartimaeus we can and will believe.

"Lord, that I may see again." Can you imagine that first moment when light again flooded this man's eyes. And not only light but a multitude of images. "Again". Bartimaeus had sight but he had lost it. So, in a very real sense, he knew the loss even more than the man born blind. Though he certainly was better off than such for at least he had a storehouse full of images that his imagination could use to people his darkness. How rich we are with the storehouse of the memory and the creativity of the imagination. Think of what life would be without them. Really it is impossible for us to get in touch with such an experience. Bartimaeus had his past experiences but he knew the loss, what he was deprived of. And he found himself reduced to the lot of a beggar.

But now, in a moment he regained his sight. What a moment! And the first thing he saw? Jesus. He must indeed have been the most beautiful of men, this man from Nazareth. He certainly had a power for attracting. Though his attractiveness was not so much in his features as in something that shone through them. When I was a boy I had difficulty understanding how my mother who was fairly short and not a beauty queen by any standards had managed to catch my father who was tall, dark and very handsome. It was only later in life I began to understand why it was that when Mom entered a room the center of focus shifted.

Our image of the God-Man is important. If it is naturally attractive it will then be one that will give emotional support to our response to him. This can be more important at some periods of our spiritual development than others but it has its importance. And it has its relevance to our relations with others, important because the second command of he Lord is like unto the first. I am a tall man. And I must confess that tall men fairly generally look down on shorter men, not only literally but in other ways as well. The fact is, Jesus was not particularly tall. We could have expected this from the generality of his people of his time even if we did not have the shroud of Turin. This was a difficulty for me. It was indeed difficult for me to imagine myself, a half-foot taller, standing with Jesus and looking down at him. Then one day I saw in the locker room a magnificent man—shorter, about Jesus' height, but so well built. Not muscled-bound by any means but a body that had been well-cared for, his circumcision very much in evidence. With my experience of this man my prejudice in regard to shorter men disappeared. This is, of course, the way we get rid of prejudice: by personally experiencing the goodness that is present in persons against whom we have been prejudiced: Jews, Blacks, gays. . . . I know I was brought up with a strong prejudice against Jews. But then a fine young Jewish man and I became very close friends, and all that evaporated. The same was my experience with gays. I can remember the day some forty years ago when I was returning from the Lido in Venice in a very crowded little ferry and I was jammed up against another young American. We began to talk. That evening we attended the opera together at the Pincheo. My new-found friend was from New York, so when I had to stay in the city I stayed with him. After a couple visits he came out of the closet and shared his gayness with me. At that time I had only the very distorted images of gays that I had collected in a very uptight theology class. But my apostolic zeal overcame my repulsions and I continued to stay with my friend—I was going to straighten him out. Well, what happened in fact was that he straightened me out; through him I came to have a wholly other image of gay men, the life they more commonly lived and what they suffered at the hands of the Church and society. Our prejudices against Jews, bearded men, shorter men, men in general, can all come into our Christ-life because of our images of Jesus.

Bartimaeus saw Jesus, a man attracting many. So much more so did he attract Bartimaeus, who now followed Jesus and in this gave glory to God.

Jesus addresses his question to each one of us: What do you want me to do for you? And it opens, like the Russian doll, to reveal within some other questions:

First of all there is the question of faith: What do I believe Jesus can do? Who is Jesus? Is he really God? Does he really have all the power of God? Can he really do anything—everything? Create and recreate? Not only heal bodies but heal minds, change minds and hearts?

What can he really do? Perhaps more difficult for some of us is the question: What do I believe Jesus is willing to do for me? Do I have very set ideas: He wants to make me holy and that means fitting me into a certain box? Am I set in my personal ideas of just what holiness is: no fun, giving up much of life, being humble, that is letting people walk all over me and not trying to get ahead using my God-given talents? The woman might add: he wants me to be subservient to the dominant male; the gay: he wants to make me straight or live a completely unrelated life. What a caricature of God! Do I believe that Jesus wants me to be fully myself, fully human, fully related and fulfilled, happier than I can conceive? As Paul put it: Eye has not seen, nor ear heard, nor has it even entered into the conception of the human mind what God has prepared for those who love him. And *now,* not some pie in the sky.

What do you want me to do for you?

We might well answer as our friend Bartimaeus: Lord, that I may see: Really see Jesus for who he is and how he feels toward me, see all reality as it really is, see Jesus in everyone, see God in all.

Lord, let me see *again.* The Lord has told us: Unless you become as a little child you will not enter in. How did we see as a child before life began to distort our vision—maybe very violently distort it through the horror of child abuse and a dysfunctional family? Then we were able to look at things with an unprejudiced openness, letting things be as they truly are, trusting in the essential goodness of people. We relied completely on the providence of God incarnated in our parents. We had imagination and vision and limitless hope, we were open to all possibilities.

Fifteen years ago, along with members of a number of other churches and a good rabbi, I created the Mastery

Foundation. I had good business men say to me more often than I liked: If I had a business with the resources and personnel of the Church and produced such meager results, I would close down tomorrow. I beheld these sleeping giants, the mainline churches, and wanted very much to wake them up. Part of that, maybe a big part of that lies in empowering the clergy and all others called to ministry in the churches. So we developed a program with the help of an expert from the bahavioral world: To Make a Difference, A Course for those who Minister. It opens to participants a very powerful and deeply spiritual experience that really makes a difference not only in their own lives but in the lives of those to whom they minister. At the beginning of the course we tell the participants: At the end of this course you can have anything that you are willing to take a stand for having got out of the course.

I think this shockingly bold statement which is nonetheless true, can be applied to our answer to the Lord's question and indeed to prayer in general. Jesus put it another way: If you say to that mountain: move, and you do not waver in your heart, it will move. When we take a stand and make a declaration we open the space for God to act, one with our freedom.

Well, what about "unanswered prayer?" Are we always to judge that the fault lies with us, that we have wavered in our hearts?

Look at Gethsemane. There is certainly no wavering heart there. "Father, let this chalice pass from me." There was total knowledge of the power of God and trust in his love. Yet there was, too, a complete acceptance of the wise disposition of the divine benignity: "Not my will but yours be done." Well indeed would it be if we added this to every prayer we uttered.

All prayer is answered. But it is not always answered in the way we expect. God looks to the heart more than to the lips. I remember one evening when we were gathered at my brother's house for dinner. His wonderful family of eight were all around the table, little Neil, then three, next to his mother. Suddenly his eyes spied the bright, shinny handle of the carving knife. Wouldn't it be fun to play with that. Fortunately mother was quicker than her little son and it was soon out of reach. Neil howled. Mother was an old meany for not letting him have the joy of playing with that bright shinny object. But if mother said "yes" to that particular "prayer," little Neil might have had the unhappiness the rest of his life of managing with only one hand. The Lord knows it is happiness we seek, for ourselves and for our loved ones. But he knows, he who sees in terms of eternal life, that what we specifically ask for is not always the way to that happiness.

What do you want me to do for you? We could—should spend hours, days, weeks, years, a lifetime answering with ever increasing insight. I went to celebrate the sacrament of reconciliation last night with my friend, Father Matthew. I like to celebrate it every week. For a "penance" Matt asked me to go sit in the "wine cellar" of the Lord and let him inebriate me with his wisdom and understanding, those precious gifts of the Spirit. Understanding—to see what "stands under"—the gift that enables us to see God in everyone and everything, present in his creative love, bringing them forth for his joy and ours. Wisdom, from the Latin word *sapientia, sapor,* savor in English: Taste and see how sweet the Lord is.

Maybe our response is adequately summed up in the words of Bartimaeus: Lord, that I may see again.

4

WHO DO YOU SAY THAT I AM?

Jesus, coming into the region of Caesarea Philippi, questioned his disciples, saying: Who do men say the Son of man is? And they said: Indeed, some say John the Baptist, and others Elijah, and others Jeremiah or one of the Prophets. He says to them: But you, who do you say that I am? And answering, Simon Peter said: You are the Christ, the Son of the living God. And answering, Jesus said to him: Blessed are you, Simon Barjona, because flesh and blood did not reveal this to you but my Father in the heavens. And I also say to you: You are Peter and on this rock I will build my church.

—Matthew 16:13–18

I didn't know if this would be the first or the last chapter that I would write—in fact it is the last—nor as I write do I still know whether I will put it at the beginning or the end of the book. Though it might find its place in the middle as it was a question Jesus asked of his Twelve in the middle of his ministry. But it surely is a fundamental question. Depending on how we answer this question, will we hear and respond to all the other questions of Jesus.

When God first appeared to Moses in the burning bush to set in motion the liberation of his people and their journey into freedom and the land of promise, this was the one question Moses asked with insistence: Who are you? Who will I say sent me? I find in my own prayer this question rising up again and again with a certain insistence: Who are you? Who are you who have such a tenacious grasp on me? Who are you, most mysterious and loving Presence? The more intimate the prayer, the more I experience God, the more this question is there: Who are you? And who am I? When I get past all the surface stuff out of which I try to construct a false self this question confronts me. Who is this "I?" I know and I believe I am truly the very image of God. O wonder of wonders! I thank you, God, for the wonder of my being. No wonder that many are content to stay on the psychiatrist's couch to keep exploring this wonder, even though such explorations rarely bring one into the experience of the true "I" who is perceived only in God in faith.

Augustine, one of the great thinkers of the Christian centuries cried out: *Noverim me ut noverim Te!* Lord, that I might know myself so that I might know You! This makes a lot of sense if I am the image of God. And yet my own experience has been the reverse. The more I have come to know God the more I have come to know myself.

I search the Scriptures. I like the way Rabbi Lawrence Kushner speaks about this:

> Somehow this "Source of all Being" [and certainly of my being] can "get through" to human beings, or at least, anyone who is listening. The result of "getting through" is what we Jews call Torah. It is, you might say, a description from "The Source of All Being" of "The Way of All Being." Trying to understand Torah constitutes the highest activity of mind, just as living in accordance with it is the highest expression of human conduct.

Of course the Rabbi's use of "The Way" immediately sets off lights within us. Jesus said: I am the Way. . . . He is our way to know God and to know ourselves in the light of our true destiny revealed to us in his Word and in prayer. Even as I hear this I hear another word of the Lord, spoken in the same discourse: "Have I been so long with you and you do not know me?"

Jesus spoke this word to one of his Twelve, though I am sure he meant it for them all. And I am sure he said it with a certain amount of pain. For this was months after the event at Caesarea Philippi.

Let us go back to that day. It had been a very busy time for Jesus. The crowds had constantly pursued him. So he headed to the northern most corner of the Lake with his Twelve. When they were there alone Jesus put the question to them: Who do people say the Son of Man is?

The disciples quickly came up with various names that were more commonly being noised about: John the Baptist, Elijah, one of the other ancient prophets. We could easily add a whole litany to these: Master, Teacher, Lord, Son of David, Son of God, the Messiah, Joseph's son, the Nazarene, the carpenter, deceiver, blasphemer. Indeed if we went on in the New Testament we could construct a very beautiful litany as it flows forth from the pen of Paul and the other inspired writers: the Saviour, the Supreme High Priest, the Mediator, the First-Born, the First and the Last, the Risen One, the Amen, the trustworthy and true Witness, the Principle of God's creation, The Beginning and the End, the Lamb who was slain, the Morning Star. . . .

And if we reach out further we find others saying: a great prophet, an enlightened teacher, a good man, a man of God, an incarnation of God. . . . This is what makes it so difficult to bring many into the fullness of the truth about Jesus, they have such beautiful partial truths. When I was first in India I was surprised to find a picture of Jesus—usually a very saccharin picture of the Sacred Heart—in many of the temples. Among the Hindus a feast is celebrated in Jesus' honor on December 24th. During such festal celebrations there is a puja in the course of which foods are set out before the one being honored. For Krishna, Ram and others this is usually chapati and rice and the like. For Jesus it might be Pepsi Cola, potato chips and even pizza. In Hindu philosophy, at least in the major schools of thought, there is but one God but he has many incarnations or manifestations. While Krishna and Ram are the manifestations for the people of India and Mohammed for the Arabs, Jesus is the incarnation for the West, so of course he would like western food. The unfortunate result of this kind of thinking is that conversion to Jesus on the part of an Indian is seen as a betrayal of one's own country and people. The unique incarnation of God in Christ Jesus is something which we can know only by faith, for there is indeed something divine in all of us who are made by God in his very own image.

But Jesus is not primarily interested in who people say that he is, in information or intellectual knowledge. Our faith ultimately cannot rest simply on what others say, even the Church. The Word we receive from the Church, from Sacred Scripture, from the living Tradition has to become a living word in us. And then, because of this experience, we can take a stand and make a declaration of faith that makes a difference.

So Jesus moves on to a more difficult and challenging question: Who do you say that I am? Jesus is putting into words the question he has always been for these men since the day they first heard him or encountered him at the Baptist's ford, on the shores of Galilee's lake or in a counting house. They looked at this man, they heard what he said, they saw what he did. No one ever spoke like him. He spoke with authority. He had dominion over the forces of nature. Who is he?

Can a person—can we really relate with a "who?"

Some years ago I had the privilege of making a Marriage Encounter. Yes, monks can make a Marriage Encounter! Any religious or priest can. The celibacy for the Kingdom to which we commit ourselves is essentially a commitment in love to Another. No human life is all that it should be unless there is at the center of it an empowering love. For most men and women this is a marital love, a marital love with God in the middle, for no human can satisfy another's aching longing for an infinite love unless he or she brings the divine love into the relationship. For the consecrated celibate this empowering love is the Lord himself, for he has invited us to be his and to be one with him in his salvific mission. During the Marriage Encounter for the celibate participant usually the chaplain of the weekend stands in for the Beloved, although another celibate participant may do so. The Encounter is a wonderful, challenging renewal of the relationship. At the end of the weekend, the couple is sent forth with a commitment to "ten and ten." Each day they are to take at least ten minutes to write a letter to their partner to let the spouse know exactly where they are and where they are in the relationship. Then, after they have exchanged the letters and have had time to read them, they spend at east ten minutes talking over what they have shared. Most marriages run into difficulty because the guy is still in love with the gal he went on the honeymoon with and doesn't know the magnificent woman at his side. And vice versa. It is precisely the wondrous realization that one's partner is an ever unfolding mystery that makes the relationship an exciting adventure all the days of our lives.

Yes, we can and we do relate with a "who." It is when we put someone in a box that we kill the relationship. That is what happened at Nazareth. The villagers knew Jesus only too well. They knew who he was: the carpenter's son, Mary's boy. And as Jesus told them, this made it impossible for them to open to a truer relationship with him, one that would have opened the space for him to bring his teaching authority and his divine power into play for their benefit. They couldn't live with this challenge to their very pat and controlled world. They had to get rid of him.

Jesus never made it easy for his Twelve. He did not hesitate to confront them. You remember the day he spoke to the people about eating his Flesh and drinking his Blood. It was too much for the crowd. They abandoned him. Then Jesus turned to the Twelve, not to give them a sacramental explanation but simply to challenge them: Will you also go away? Peter began to show his leadership then: Lord, to whom shall we go. You have the words of eternal life.

Again at Caesarea Philippi Jesus was not just asking them for their thoughts, ideas, opinions. He was asking them, and us, where do we stand: Who do you say . . . ? What is your declaration in faith? This was the magnificence of Peter here. He was taking a very clear stand: You are the Christ, the Anointed One, the Messiah, the Son of the living God. What a magnificent declaration. There was no ambiguity here.

I really love Peter. I wrote a book about him. If God could make a saint out of this man he can make a saint out of anyone. He was a loud-mouthed, bossy, braggart, who more often than not put his foot into his mouth. Sure, he would walk on water—for about twenty seconds. The instance I enjoy the most is the day he brashly affirmed that his Master paid the temple tax. Jesus took him to task and gave him a salutary penance. The great fisherman, the captain of the crew, had to get out a little line and go down like any five-year-old and cast in his line and wait for a bite. I can just see the rest of the Twelve standing around, making great sport of this humiliating experience: "Have you caught anything yet, Peter?" But we don't want to miss the fact that right in the middle of this Jesus gives extraordinary expression to his special attachment to Peter, for here we find the one instance in the Gospels where Jesus says "us" referring to himself and a human person, and that person is Peter.

On this occasion at Caesarea Philippi, Peter comes through. But Jesus makes it very clear: he comes though because Jesus' own Father has enlightened him and has given him the grace to move with that enlightenment. It is a great moment for this chosen man. His life's mission is clearly affirmed. He is to be the bedrock of Jesus' Church. Without Peter we do not have the Church of Jesus Christ.

Yes, Peter went on to fail Jesus terribly. He not only ran away like the rest of the apostles. But when he plucked up his courage—shamed undoubtedly by the memory of his usual boastful bravado earlier in the evening—his courage quickly melted before the onslaughts of a humble serving girl. Oh, what little courage we humans have! But failure does not undo our declaration. When we take a stand and make a declaration, we open a space to be what we declare. We may fail but the space remains and we can get up and go on. I am a biped. I do fall down at times. But I don't then crawl for the rest of my life. No, I get up and

go on walking because "I am a biped." It was Peter's declaration that led him quickly to tears. The declaration
stood and was there as he ran to the tomb, as he received
one of the first personal encounters with the risen Lord,
as he was challenged to move on to an even more auda-
cious declaration by the risen Lord: Do you love me more
than these?

Jesus asked. And Peter took a stand. Most of us don't
dare ask even our closest friend: Who do you say that I
am? Yet it is the fundamental question that lies at the bottom of every human commitment to relationship, be it in
friendship, marriage or religious or monastic community.
It is the question that lies at the bottom of all spiritual
accompaniment (I don't like the expression "spiritual
direction." It is an expression that came late to the Church,
during the more rationalist age when spiritual programs
got laid out in detail and one needed someone to direct
one through the maze of the castle or up the winding
mountain trail. The danger is that we are influenced by
the words we use. A spiritual director can begin to direct,
forgetting that for us there is in truth only one director:
Holy Spirit, and the role of the spiritual guide, whom we
more traditionally call spiritual mother or father, imply-
ing a fullness able to engender life, is to help hear what
the Spirit is saying, how she is leading.). We want and
need someone to reflect back to us as clearly and fully as
possible just who we are. To see ourselves clearly in the
mirror of the eyes of another, especially one whose love for
us allows that one to intuitively see what others fail to see,
one whose faith enlightened by the Spirit's gift of understanding—to see what stands under—what a tremendous
gift and grace. Unfortunately, *quid quid recipitur per
modum recipientis recipitur* (the only Latin phrase I

remember from my years of studying Saint Thomas' *Summa theologiae:* Whatever is received is received according to the mode of the receiver.). Others have only a limited perception of us and many have us boxed in. Perception can be colored by jealousy, competition, envy, pride, hurt, etc. We need to receive such perceptions with caution. They can undermine us and keep us from knowing our own true magnificence as divinized Christ persons, beloved of God and gifted by God. True affirmation we long for and can be immensely helped by it. But unfortunately it is rare in a world which is extremely competitive and where most are intent on building up and preserving their own false self.

We used to have a "chapter of faults." First each member of the community was given the opportunity to declare any faults he was aware of having committed and he was given a salutary penance, Then the brethren were invited to proclaim any faults they had perceived in another. The one proclaimed—and I can tell you it was often frater Basil—would then prostrate and stay there until the superior told him he could rise. He was then given an admonition and due penance. It was supposed to help us grow in humility and self-knowledge. And I suppose in some ways it did as brothers, supposedly in charity, pointed out our faults before the whole community. But in the renewal we dropped this practice without hesitation because I think the common consensus was that it did more harm than good. We came to see that almost all already had a low enough opinion of themselves or too low. What was more needed, and in fact actually did more to foster charity, was affirmation. We have yet to develop a regular "chapter of affirmation" but support groups instinctively do this if they are true support groups.

It is provocative that Jesus asks his question halfway through his formative and intimate time with these men. He had given them a good bit of data to go by. They still had a lot to learn. But in the end, as he tells Peter, it is not flesh and blood, not human experience that gives them the answer to this question but the Father in heaven: No one knows the Son but the Father.

Perhaps the disciples had themselves labored through all the opinions that they expressed in responding to Jesus' first question, either on their own or in conversation with their companions. How good it was to be part of that chosen support group and not a lone disciple. We all want to find or create a faith sharing group that can support us on the journey. Otherwise it is a much more difficult and always challenged journey in an alien and largely faithless world. It is in fact a lifetime labor to answer this most basic of questions. Once we have made our declaration as we move along our responses may not vary but our understanding of them certainly does if we are growing as human and divinized persons living in relationship with this Man-God.

Strange isn't it: the disciples themselves never asked Jesus: Who are you? But then, how often have we asked the Lord to tells us, reveal to us who he is. We don't like to reveal our ignorance. We like to pretend and often act as if we have all the answers. That was the evil of the little catechism—for all its virtues, whatever they might have been for us—it fostered a sense that we had the answers. Such certainly did not foster an open relationship with this Man-God. One of the elements that keeps a relationship alive is the enticing mystery of the person and the hope of discovering more of what really makes this person tick.

Undoubtedly part of what underlies the importance of this question for us is the question: Who am I? What really makes me tick? We are fellow humans. If I can understand the other better then I should hopefully understand myself better. And see more clearly my way to happiness and fulfillment. *Noverim te ut noverim me.*

The Twelve may have not asked the question because by this time they well suspected if they did dare ask the question: Who are you? his answer would have been couched in words or even in a parable that would have opened more questions than it answered. He wanted to spur them and us on to the growth that comes from living in the question.

In the end I have to hear the Lord say to me: Who, Basil, do you say that I am?

Who are you, Lord?

—You are my Friend: you have given the greatest sign of this, you have laid down your life for me. You understand me. You have lived through what I have lived through as a growing male. We share the same hopes for yourself and myself. You are the real rock and anchor of my life.

—You are my Teacher: I come to you. I believe you are Truth. I am confident that at your own pace you will teach me all that I need to now.

—You are my God: I don't know how to put it all together, Friend and God, but I accept it. I adore. I rest in the mystery. I long to know and, more important, to experience.

—You are my Saviour: you have brought me in many way ways and at many levels out of my blind, stupid, enslaving, self-centered, frightening, miserable, lonely sinfulness. You make up for all my failures. You are glorified in this. You give me hope of final and complete redemption, freedom to be who I am to be, to be all love.

I want you to be my Joy: joy in who you are, in the glory that is yours, in the joy that is yours.

You are my joy!

5

WILL GOD GRANT JUSTICE
TO HIS CHOSEN?

And Jesus told them a parable to the effect that it
behooved them to pray always and not to go unconscious. He said: There was in a certain city a certain
judge who feared not God nor had regard for others.
And there was a widow in that city who came to the
judge saying: Give me justice in the face of my oppo-
nent. And for a time he would not. But after her petitions he said to himself: If indeed I fear not God nor
have regard for others, at least because of the trouble
this widow causes me I will give her justice lest in the
end she wears me out with her coming. And the Lord
said: Hear what the unjust judge says. And will not
God grant justice to his chosen ones crying to him day
and night? And be patient with them? He will quickly
give them justice. Nonetheless, when the Son of Man
comes will he find faith on the earth?

—Luke 18:1–8

This is in a way a rather astounding story or parable
that Jesus tells us here. He dares to liken God to an
unjust judge, a man who is a law unto himself and doesn't
care what God thinks nor what any one else thinks. It
sounds almost blasphemous. If Jesus hadn't done it, we
certainly would not dare to do it. Yet as the early Church
sang, he is the one who did not cling to his divine prerog-
atives but emptied himself to become one with us. If it
will help us to understand what he is trying to teach us,

51

he is ready to cast himself in the guise of an corrupt judge. And he seems to say no matter how little faith we have in the divine goodness and mercy, if we keep pestering the Lord with our petitions, we will get what we want: Ask and you shall receive.

Unfortunately, it is true that many do have an image of God as a stern judge who is a law unto himself, has little regard for us in our pain, and is, indeed, unjust. It comes out of the story of their own lives or out of the lives of others. Think of the handicapped, maimed from birth. With no fault on their part, they are condemned to a life of suffering and deprivation, often looked down upon, despised and rejected. Is this just? I have a great nephew who was born with some brain damage. Walking, balance was always difficult for him but then seizures began, some days as many as thirty. This innocent, bright, cheery little boy—where's the justice? Happily, in his case delicate brain surgery freed him from much of his affliction. But he might well ascribe that to the brilliance of a dedicated and caring doctor without going beyond that to the provident Source.

Think of the homosexual: God made me this way and according to his Church I can't have intimacy, the full expression of my love, have my love celebrated and honored in marriage. His Church says the love my partner and I have is inferior to that which my brother and his wife have and is not worthy of celebrating or blessing.

Is God just?

The prophets of old stated the case rather bluntly. God is the potter and we are the clay. He can make out of us whatever he wants; he can do with us whatever he wants. His dominion is complete.

But is this the whole story?

Jesus speaks here of God's "chosen ones." He was above all the Chosen One. Both at his baptism and in the moments of heavenly glory on Tabor, a Voice from on high proclaimed it. Of this Chosen One God asked not only that he should suffer as a child because of the cruelty and sin of others—born in a stable, a displaced person, quickly forced into exile—but his was a life of poverty and hard work, followed by a ministry that brought upon him suspicion, hatred, persecution and finally a most painful and ignominious death.

Why? Why did it have to be done this way? In a way it tells us of a love beyond all telling—a mystery of love. This is, of course, the bottom line: love. And anything that will help us to grow in love is ultimately good. A man who saw into this more deeply than most of us said: For those who love God all things work together unto good. To be asked, to be chosen, to be called to share in the saving mission of Christ, to fill up what is wanting in the passion of Christ (to use again the words of that insightful and inspired man, Paul) is a great privilege, a great grace. Yet the question still stands: Why this way? God is free. From his freedom comes all our freedom. He can justly have it any way he wants. But we can still ask: Why? In fact, whether we want it or not, the why rises up out of our depths. And while we can catch glimpses of an answer, in the end we have to accept the reality—which is humility—that we don't fully understand, we don't see. We live with the question and humbly to the best of our ability with the help of his grace say "yes" to the mystery. Isaiah's words are not too consoling sometimes but they are nonetheless true:

> My thoughts are not your thoughts
>   Nor your ways my ways, says the Lord,

> For as high as the heavens are above the earth.
> So are my ways above your ways
> > And my thoughts above your thoughts.

In our afflictions, no matter who or what are the secondary causes, it is the Lord calling us to a greatness with his Son, his Chosen One. This can indeed be a hard saying, easier for one looking in from the outside to say or hear. It is OK to sweat blood; his Chosen One did in Gethsemane.

Jesus asks a rhetorical question: Will not God grant justice? And he quickly responds that God will quickly respond, yes, he will grant them justice. But Jesus brings a couple other ideas into the equation: God's patience and our faith.

God has to be patient with us because we really do not understand who God is and who we are. God is God, the Creator, the Source, the Lord. There is nothing else in our experience like unto this Reality. Maybe the nearest thing to it is the dominion current legislation seeks to give to a woman over the life and being of the child who lives within her, allowing her to bring it to birth or allowing her, by her own free choice, to dispose of the child, depriving the little one of all joy, of the potential and the wonder of a human life. The killing, so euphemistically called "mercy killing," moves in the same direction. If we in our conceptualization can give one creature such arbitrary control over the fate of another creature because she is a participant in the creation of that child, why should we have any difficulty giving the Creator such a free choice in what he does with his creatures? There is an infinite difference between Creator and creature, between the sourcing of life on the part of the Creator and the creature he allows to participate in his creative act. He has every right to circumscribe the freedom of his participant. And if we are rational we can see the full rationality of such a circumscription when it is to respect the right to life, liberty and the pursuit of happiness of another.

Jesus has made our position very clear. He has told us point blank: Without me you can do nothing. In theory we readily assent to this word. He is the vine, we are the branches; we draw all our sustenance from him. We cannot live without him, not to speak of producing fruit, of having a fruitful life. But in practice how do we act and how do we think? Total dependence is our actuality; independence is our preferred mode. This is certainly one of the lessons of this little parable. The widow knew that there was only one way by which she could get justice. She knew her complete dependence on the judge, just or unjust. And this clear knowledge fuelled her prayer. So Jesus asks: Will he find faith? Will there be anyone who really believes that we are totally dependent upon God and on Jesus as our saviour.

We do not like to be dependent. Let's be honest. How much of our prayer really comes out of a realization of total dependence? How often do we go through the motions of prayer because it is the right and proper thing to do, even while we feel we have everything under control? As we stood in our pews at Mass last Sunday did we have any sense that our continued existence at that very moment depended on God's benignity, on his continued mercy and goodness?

Getting hold of this reality, then doesn't the question of the justice of God take on another color? When all that we have, all that we are is at every moment largess and mercy, how can we speak of any right in justice toward the source of that goodness?

There is a story Jesus tells that seems to rankle us a bit, or maybe more than a bit. Jesus told of a man who had a big vineyard. He went out in the early morning and hired every man he could find to work in his vineyard and they mutually agreed on the going wage for a day's work. Later the owner went out again and he spied more workers and immediately he hired them. And so it happened again and again through the day. And even as evening came on he found some more and hired them. When the day's labor came to a halt, the owner ordered his paymaster to give each and every worker a day's pay. He may have had various reasons for this. He may have been thinking of the morrow and wanting them all to come back. Or he may have been a man with a deep sense of social justice and compassion and knew that each worker needed a day's pay to provide for himself and his family. Whatever be his motive, each was to receive a day's wage. So the fellow who worked only an hour in the cool of the evening got the same as the man who had wearied his back and was soaked with sweat from a full day's work. Where's the justice? We spontaneously cry out with the poor, weary fellow who worked the whole day long. We are very prone to equate justice with equality. I think that comes to play here for us. But more, we are prone to begin to think we have a right to what is given in sheer mercy, benignity, largess.

Faith in its fullness grasps that all is gift. And God is very patient with us as we so slowly come to realize that. The little story of the judge and widow speaks a good bit about justice: He is the unjust judge. She cries for justice. He decides to give her justice. But this is all in the translation, a good translation but perhaps misleading. The Greek speaks rather of vindication. The woman can indeed be asking that her faith in God's mercy in the face of the evil one is what is to be vindicated. And the judge is more properly described as "unrighteous"—one who is not right, does not live up to the norms.

In any case, parables should not be pushed too far. Not every detail of them is applicable at every level of the opening out of the Word. Luke tells us that the primary reason Jesus told this particular story was to teach us that it behoves us to pray always and not to go unconscious. It is not only that we are never to forget our total dependence and are therefore never to cease imploring the gift of life, that our faith in the All-merciful and All-good One might be vindicated. It is the value of persistence in prayer.

Jesus brought home this same lesson on another occasion. Not so much by word as by action. The similarities are striking. Again it is the persistent woman. Again Jesus let's himself be painted in darker colors. They were in alien territory, in the region of Tyre and Sidon. A Canaanite woman, a Greek says Mark, came to Jesus to plead for her little daughter, who was grievously tormented. The poor, innocent, little one. You can imagine how heart-rending was the plea of the mother. And yet Jesus pretended to turn a deaf ear to her pleading. So persistent was this woman's cries that even Jesus' disciples became her advocates: Give her what she wants because she keeps shouting after us. Even to them his reply sounds rather ethnic, full of haughty superiority. But as the woman persists Jesus speaks directly to her in a way that really shocks us. He speaks of this poor grovelling mother with words that sound absolutely brutal. He literally calls her and her child dogs. This may not have been so shocking to the disciples who surrounded him, at least not the way it shocks us. But maybe by a reverse reaction he was trying to bring them to their senses and help them realize that the attitude that the Jews at that time entertained towards the gentiles was indeed offensive. I recently spent eight years in China. Among the Chinese there are the people of the Middle Kingdom, the Han, who traditionally are the purest and most ancient line. They possess, rightly, an immense pride in their five-thousand-year-old civilization. But with this came a sense of looking down upon others, an attitude that came into their language and has remained there. So in regards to other Chinese a terminology is used that speaks of them as dogs. And foreigners are "foreign-devils." The terminology is a carryover from ancient times, but the terms we use do have a formative influence on our mentality and attitudes. This is why we are making such an effort in our times to purge our usage of words and expressions that arise from past mentalities that are less than worthy of our human family: sexist language, patriarchal language, pejorative expressions in regard to different ethnic groups and so on. It is not easy to change a widely used language overnight but we do need to be sensitive and make the effort.

When we are driven by a strong faith and desire we are not going to be put off by language. We cut through it to grasp the reality we want. In spite of the put-down, and even turning it to her advantage, this woman showed the power of persistent prayer. That very moment—no delay here—her daughter was healed.

When the Son of Man comes will he find such faith on the earth? We hope so. It is his gift. For it we pray—the fullness of faith that trusts unconditionally, that opens to unconditional love.

There is a God. And he is good.

6

IS IT LAWFUL . . . ?

Jesus entered again into a synagogue. And there was there a man having a hand that was withered. They watched Jesus carefully. If on the Sabbath he would heal the man, they might accuse him. Jesus says to the man with the dried up hand: Rise, stand in the middle. And Jesus says to them: Is it lawful on the Sabbath to do good or to do evil, to save life or to destroy? But they were silent. And looking around at them with anger, greatly grieved at the hardness of their heart, Jesus says to the man: Stretch forth the hand. And he stretched it forth, his hand was restored. The Pharisees, going out, immediately entered into counsel with the Herodians against Jesus that they might destroy him.

—Mark 3:1–6

As we hear this story we can feel the tension of the scene entering into our own bones. Jesus, flashing with anger, making a whip of cord and driving the cheating dealers out of the Temple, that we can more readily understand. But the cold, almost fierce anger that quietly exuded from Jesus as he confronted the hypocrisy of the ruling Pharisees is chilling. It is as though something of the coldness of their proud and haughty hearts had seeped into the Lord. But, not so. For immediately Mark goes on to tell us: Jesus grieved at the hardness of their hearts. This is how righteous anger differs from self-righteous anger, this accompanying feeling of pain and sorrow for the sad plight of the ones with whom we are angry. Indeed we are not angry with them but with what they are doing. For them in love we feel grief that they could so act or be entrapped in the prejudice, blindness or stupidity that holds them.

Is it lawful . . . ? In a way we are surprised to hear Jesus ask such a question. After all, he is God, the Lawgiver himself, above the Law certainly and free to change the Law in any way he wants. Yet this is part of the fullness of the incarnation. Jesus entered into our humanity not in some universal or abstract way, but very concretely. He became a man among women and men of a certain place and time, a certain culture and religious heritage. He respected that and entered into it. As he said, he didn't come to do away with the established Law. He came to fulfill it and to help us to understand how to interpret and use Law for the purpose which he as God gave it. Jesus had no problem with the Law or a legal system as such. It was a legalism and ritualism that shackled people that called forth his anger. The Sabbath, the holiest and most respected observance of the Law, was made for us, not we for it.

What is particularly angering here is the way these men are using a fellow human, exploiting a man who is already suffering from being despised by many. They had no care for this brother in his pain and need. They were only intent upon their own jealous schemes. It is enough to make any good person *very* angry.

And Jesus was angry. And at the same time he was grieved. So great is his goodness and compassion. He actually loved these malicious Pharisees and he would die for them as much as for you and me. He grieved that the hardness of their heart would not allow the saving grace of Calvary to penetrate, heal and make whole, that they might be warmed by the Spirit and filled with her joy.

We can see how rich a man was Jesus in the fullness of his emotional life. He let a strong, what we tend to call virile anger well up in him. It was something fierce. And at the same time there was grief, sorrow, pain and compassion not only for the poor victim who stood there in a rather hopeless state but also for the keen-eyed Pharisees who were maliciously watching his every move. Every human emotion of itself is good. We can celebrate that we are feeling men and women. But we are not just feelers—no matter how important this is and men generally need to get more in touch with this—we are endowed with rationality, the power and responsibility to judge and moderate how we will use our feelings. In this instance Jesus did not judge it was best to use that choleric energy to strike out. Rather he let it give a certain sharpness to the rational discourse to which he invited his adversaries: Is it lawful. . . . ?

Is it lawful . . . ? Jesus was going more than halfway with them. He was meeting them on their own ground. These Pharisees prided themselves on knowing and keeping the Law. Little persons who dare not follow their dreams and attempt great things, take refuge in being the legalist and keeping every jot and title and thus making claim to being superior to others, especially those charismatic types who dare to go beyond the Law and do their striking deeds, good though they may be. Yes, these Pharisees knew the Law—the letter of the Law. And hadn't a clue or blinded themselves from seeing any clue of what, in the Divine Legislators's intent, the Law is all about. Moreover they in their arrogance "improved" upon the Divine and hedged all about God's Law with many of their own perceptive interpretations.

Well, Jesus would use a question, a question in the field of their own supposed expertise to see if he could not possibly make a crack in the hard shell that enclosed their hearts in the hope of slipping in. Jesus brought the particular precept involved here, and in so doing all particular precepts, back to the basic context in which it must be placed to be rightly interpreted: good and evil, salvation and destruction. Any interpretation we make of the Divine Law, of the laws of the Church—which are supposed to exist only to further the Divine Law—that leads to evil or destruction is obviously a false and erroneous interpretation. The Divine Law and all ecclesiastical law must be interpreted in a way that serves goodness and salvation.

In this light the Pharisees and their interpretations were immediately and patently condemned. To interpret the Sabbath in a way that left a man shackled by a deformed limb was clearly a desecration. On another occasion Jesus would state it more sharply. Here in his grief and pain over these Pharisees he is only trying to make some opening into their hearts.

Alas, this is the most astounding outcome of this encounter. Not the man's instantaneous restoration but the action of the Pharisees, How blind our prejudice can make us. Or our defensiveness when we are trying to preserve our own territory, so to speak. These men have just seen Divine power work a first-class miracle and what do they do? They give no consideration at all to this wonder. Their own plan has been thwarted. So they seek allies who can further their ends, allies who until now have been hated enemies, enemies of their people and all they stand for. This blindness to reality, this total self-centered subjectivity, is astonishing. And the lengths to which it is willing to go: allies with enemies and out-right murder. It is astonishing until we stop to take a good look at how we have sometimes so completely betrayed what we stand for and what we have so long worked for. In the heat of a passionate moment we have used and abused and in so doing have killed the Christ within us and in our sisters and brothers.

Is it lawful . . . is not a bottom-line question. But the use of it by Jesus and our own use of it signals the danger-ous territory we are in when we fall back on it. Law is good—in context, the proper context giving birth to the proper interpretation. In our saner moments we are more concerned with the context. There lies our questions: is it good, does it save life. Unfortunately in many places today it is "lawful" by civil law, a law that betrays itself, to kill the unborn but it certainly is not good, it does not save life. Life, as even our United States forefathers saw: life, lib-erty and the pursuit of happiness, is the bottom line. Without life and liberty we can never pursue true happi-ness. And for this God made us: to share God's happiness. True law and any valid interpretation of law must serve life and freedom. Only then is it good, calling us to do good.

Sometimes the situation makes the true interpreta-tion patently clear, as in this Gospel case. Sometimes, however, it is not so clear. The common good which the law primarily serves can be in dynamic tension with the personal good of an individual. Sacrifice of some good becomes necessary. I don't think we can always make an *a priori* judgment in favor of the common good. Sometimes it is only the strength that is drawn from others at their cost that enables a member to survive.

A legalistic community may look good on the outside. Everything is in good order. But Jesus always described his Church as a net full of good and bad fish, a field of wheat oversewn with weeds. At best a rather messy sort of collection. No West Point image here. And it was to continue this way until the harvest. Saint Paul gives us the challenging word: For those who love God all things work together unto good. The bad fish, the weeds have their role to play. And yet our Lord did speak of cutting out the scandalizing member, even one as important as the eye. What is the true call of law, what is the ultimate good, what serves life? We need to live in the space of these questions as we make our way in the Way, seeking the Truth that is eternal Life.

7

WHY DO YOU NOT BELIEVE?

Jesus compelled the disciples to get into the boat and to go ahead of him to the other side. . . . The boat was not many yards from the land. It was tossed about by the waves for there was a contrary wind. In the fourth watch of the night Jesus came toward them walking on the sea. And the disciples seeing him walking on the sea were frightened. They cried out: It is a ghost. But Jesus immediately spoke to them: Be at peace. It is I. Don't be afraid. Answering him, Peter said: Lord, if it is you, command me to come to you on the waters. And Jesus said: Come. And getting out of the ship, Peter walked on the waters and came toward Jesus. But experiencing the wind he became fearful and beginning to sink, he cried out: Lord, save me. And immediately Jesus, stretching out his hand, took hold of him, and said to him: Little-faith, why do you not believe? And they got into the ship and the wind ceased. Those in the ship worshiped Jesus saying: Truly you are the Son of God.

—Matthew 14:22–33

No, I haven't tried walking on water. I'd much rather be in water, swimming. And I am sure that that is not only because I like swimming so much. When I am swimming I feel I am in control of the situation. I am a good swimmer. I was a lifeguard. And yet I must admit, there are the fears.

Some memories stand out for me. When I was a boy I was swimming in an old quarry. The water was perfectly clear, a beautiful green, and very cold. My friend was only twenty feet away. And then suddenly he was not there. They finally brought up his body two days later.

More traumatic was a later experience. I was in Israel. I was working on a book on Saint Bernard with a professor from the University of Tel Aviv to honor Bernard's 900th birthday. After we finished our work I rented a car and set out to experience some of the places I had heard about all my life in the Gospels. One morning I found myself in a kibbutz on the shores of the Sea of Galilee. I got up early and went out for a swim. As I approached the swimming area I saw a sizeable group of Palestinians gathered on the beach so I decided to wait. I went off a bit and sat by the side of the water. I opened my Bible and began to read of Jesus walking here and calling his disciples: Come! I will make you fishers of men and women. As I read an old Palestinian came close by. He was looking out over the water and weeping. When I perceived that most of the group on the beach had left and that one of them was now in the water, repeatedly diving off the raft, I decide it was time to go in. As I got up and headed toward the beach the old man spoke to me: My son drowned. My heart cramped: This poor man. No wonder he weeps. But I thought he spoke of an event long past for he was very old. He followed me and as we approached the beach he said to the few still there: He'll find. He'll find. I put on my goggles and prepared to dive in; what he was saying had not yet registered with me. I dove deep and stroked my way along the bottom. Then I could hardly believe what I saw: A boy, as it were crawling on the bottom. He didn't know how to swim and had got in over his head. His body was rigid for he had drowned the day before around noon. With great sorrow this "fisher of men" brought this boy, an only son of thirteen years, to his grief stricken father. I had to spend some hours in the sea later that day to make friends again with water. And now each time I launch out into the deep I am very aware that at any moment it all could come to an end.

Many prefer to stay in the supposed security of he boat. But there are those who want more. And hear a call: Come. They want to enter into the mystical depths of a Bernard or Mechtilde. Or go forth into the challenges of the missions like Ricci or de Nobile. Or face the challenges of injustice like an Oscar Romero or a Meg McKenna. Or be with the poorest of the poor like a Dorothy Day or Frederick Ozanam. Or to raise one's children for heaven like Zele and Louis Martin. And though we may launch out with enthusiasm, so few of us keep our eyes on the Lord. We begin to make judgments in the light of our own resources and soon we are sinking, if not all the way into depression and despair at least into a certain mediocrity that settles for something less—for our own effortful swimming rather than a walk with the Divine.

Why do we doubt?

Jesus has told us that unless we become as little ones we will not enter in. When your three-year-old comes running up to you, asking for something, do you think she gives any thought of whether she deserves it or has done something to earn it. No, she is fully confident as to your bounty and benignity and that confidence spills over into her expectation.

We don't believe in part because we think we have to earn or deserve what we get. Digging a little deeper we see that this is the case because we want to stand on our own two feet and not be beholding. More deeply yet, we are caught in the false self, that self that is made up of what I do, what I have, what others think of me. I want to be able to say I have it, yes, even God gives it to me, because of what I have done. The sophistication of pride is here—and ingratitude.

This is another root of our not believing: our ingratitude. When we stop and take stock of what the Lord has already done for us, given us, is giving us, there can be no doubt as to his bounty and benignity. What have I that I have not received? Yet I take it all so much for granted and think I have a right to rail against heaven when the Lord withdraws any of the gifts I have so presumptiously used for years without ever a thought of thanksgiving. My fingers now go racing across the keys of the computer. How tragic it would be if suddenly even just one of these two hands fell limp and could no longer strike the keys or perform the many, many tasks it does for me each day, each hour. Yet how often have I stopped to thank the Lord for the marvel of this hand, the way it does operate, the way my mind and my eye can direct it, the way it can be trained so that it leaps from one key to another with a certain sureness and speed. I thank you Lord for my hand, my head, my heart, my whole being. When we go further and allow ourselves to get in touch with the gift God has given us in the life and death of Jesus, how could we ever doubt the benignity, the good will of our God toward us. As Jesus pointed out, if we poor sinners know how to be good to our children, how much more the Father in heaven?

There is yet another factor that undermines the confident expectation of our faith. And it is the fact that not only do we not want to be dependent recipients but we really do not want to be able to walk on the water. Priests and bishops are more concerned about how they look than about bringing the light and consolation of the faith to the poor. Parents are more concerned about raising their children for success in this world than that those children become saints. We contemplatives are taken up with our immediate doings and don't want to be lost in ecstasy. Note the word we use: "lost"—we don't believe that it is only in God we find our true self. What we fear is the loss of that false self we build up by our doings.

Why do I not believe? What can I do about it?

I don't give the Lord all the opportunity I should to make his goodness and love known to me. I will be a person of lectio and prayer. Each day I will sit down with the Lord in his inspired Word and let him speak to me and reveal himself to me. I will talk honestly and straightforwardly with him. And let him do the same.

I not only take so much for granted; I act as if I were the source. I will be a person of thanksgiving. From the moment I wake up in the morning, my word will be "thank you:" Thank you, Lord, for a good night's sleep. Thank you, Lord, for a new day. Thank you, Lord, for a warm and comfortable bed. Thank you, Lord, for the roof over my head. Thank you, Lord, for your presence here with me. Thank you, Lord, for the strength and ability to get up out of this bed, to exercise my muscles, to walk. Thank you, Lord, for this shower, this hot water, this soap, these towels, this wonderful body of mine which you give into my care and use. Thank, you, Lord. . . . Can we ever stop? And I know from my own experience: when we are in the thank-you mode we enjoy each thing so much more and so much more consciously.

This seems like it would be something easy enough to do. But in fact it demands even as it creates a profoundly different mind set or mentality from that which most commonly prevails in us. It demands that kind of humility that authentically accepts reality in its fullness. Jesus put it this way: Without me you can do nothing. God is the source of all that is. We are totally dependent on his largesse. Fully accepting this means the death of the false self, that projection which we seek to create out of our own doings and havings. It means the freedom to be my true self and to celebrate this gift of God to me and to everybody else. Indeed, it is the only thing I can give others that has true worth: my true self. It means living in the domain of complete freedom, joy and peace, because I no longer have to create myself but live in the bounty of a God of limitless bounty and benignity.

Why do I not believe?

Lord, I do believe; help my unbelief.

8

DO YOU BELIEVE THAT I CAN DO THIS FOR YOU?

Jesus moving on was followed by two blind men crying out and saying: Pity us, Son of David! As Jesus entered the house the blind men approached and he says to them: Do you believe that I can do this for you? They say to him: Yes, Lord. Then he touched their eyes, saying: According to your faith let it be done to you. And their eyes were opened. And Jesus spoke earnestly to them: See that you let no one know. But they, going out, talked about him in all that land.

—Matthew 9:27–31

This is a very interesting little story here. Jesus has just worked a number of miracles, one proving he could forgive sins, a divine prerogative as his protagonists pointed out; another, one of his greatest, the restoration to life of Jairus' daughter. It is no wonder then that these two blind men come chasing after him. Yet Jesus turns a deaf ear. He is heading "home"—the house in Capernaum which served as his home base. One gets the sense that he is tired. He tells his disciples that something went out of him when the afflicted woman reached through the crowd and touched the edge of his cloak with faith. Working miracles is not an easy task for our humanity. The Divine power that surges through us takes its toll. Jesus just wants to get home and have some quiet restful time.

But these two come after him. And they will not be shaken off. Even when he enters the house they come in after him. Finally Jesus has to face the issue. Again, we are left with an impression. It seems when Jesus is approached with faith he cannot say "no." Do you believe I can do this? To their strong, bold affirmation, Jesus' response is: According to your faith let it be done to you.

Any prayer of petition we make to the Lord is always answered. And this is the answer: Do you believe I can do this? We sometimes feel our prayer has not been heard or has not been answered. It has, but to the answer of Jesus: Do you believe I can do this, we have consciously or more likely unconsciously responded: No—not really. Or: Yes, but I don't believe you will do it for me. Or something like: Others say you can. Or: I think so. Do I believe Jesus can really make me holy, make me patient, make me chaste, make me sober? Can he do this for a poor, weak, stupid, back-sliding, self-indulgent sinner like me? We have to respond out of our own faith experience. Then Jesus' further response is: According to your faith let it be done to you. This is why there is apparently no answer. Jesus does respond according to our faith and our faith is not there. Jesus respects us. We have our role to play. Every work of the Lord in us is a collaborative effort: his divine action finding room to act in us to the extent we give it room, that we are open to it by our faith. Nonetheless Jesus does more than his part. Here he touches the eyes of these two. The divine touch. Even as Jesus asks about our faith he reaches out to touch us, to reassure us of his presence, his care, his concern, his gentleness.

There is something wonderful about human touch. We all have a terrible body-hunger. We want and need to be touched. When someone touches us with a loving touch it says volumes; it satisfies something deep within us. Today Jesus often touches us through others, our and his fellow humans. And there are also those wondrous interior touches. To experience the benefit from them, the joy and healing of them, we have to be sensitive to them. Maybe our prayer of petition always needs to be accompanied by that of the public official: I believe, Lord, help my unbelief. Touch me. Give me the experience so that I can respond to your question: Do you believe, with a wholehearted and total: Yes.

These were two. How good it was that they had each other. Undoubtedly it was in good part this mutual support that enabled them to persevere in their pursuit of Jesus and his healing power in the face of a seeming "no" on Jesus' part. Jesus didn't even seem to acknowledge their presence. As with the Syro Phoenician woman they were being challenged to greater faith in his goodness and benignity. Perhaps they had heard his story about the widow keeping after the unjust judge. But they urged each other on—probably not so much in words as in the actual doing, in pursuing Jesus together.

This solidarity pleased the heart of Jesus, He would say: Where two are gathered in my name, there I am. And these two cried out together his messianic name, so powerfully meaningful for these Jews: Son of David. And their prayer was not each for himself alone. They were praying for each other. Jesus says: Whenever two agree on anything, it will be done for them. The love, care and support these two had for each other could not be denied. There eyes were opened! They saw. Were they surprised? No—not with their faith, not with Jesus' gentle touch. Just delighted.

How unreasonable Jesus' word to them sounds: See that you let no one know. Really impossible. They may have been strangers in town and could slip away. But certainly wherever they called home, everyone would know. Or was this implicitly a call to a life apart? These men had a strong faith. Now their eyes were open. They saw Jesus. They experienced his touch. Were they being invited to an interior life—to be leaven, silently, lovingly, prayerfully supporting the growth of Jesus' life in all, not by preaching or an active ministry but by a more powerful life apart of prayer, praise and thanksgiving. As great as their faith was, their response to this special call, to a contemplative way of being was not there. The contemplative way is a very special one. Perhaps one of the demands of it that is most difficult is not giving in to the powerful urge in us to go out and proclaim the wondrous goodness of our God. Everything in us impels us in this direction. And it seems so right and righteous. Didn't Mary sing her *Magnificat?* But the Lord's call is to go within and be praise and thanksgiving.

Many are called, few are chosen. Again and again in the Gospels we hear Jesus challenge those who he has touched in a special healing way not to broadcast what he has done. What does he expect? We see it in the incident of the healing of the ten lepers. He expects worship and thanksgiving, praise and appreciation. This is the role of the contemplative among the People of God (Are they to be just one out of ten?) Certainly it is only by a special touch of the Lord that one would even think of such a role. Touched, our eyes are opened. We see Jesus and his goodness and hear the often at first incomprehensible call: not to tell, not to go forth to all nations, but quietly celebrate the mercies of the Lord, to be a living thanksgiving. Again it is time to hear the question: Do you believe I can do this for you? Can I give you Mary's better part? The response has to be one of very daring faith to say "yes" to such a beautiful, special and intimate vocation.

Let us take a bit of time or more. Let us listen to all the aspirations of our heart. This is what God hears—not so much the words of our mouths. Aspirations not only for ourselves personally, for our family and friends, but our aspirations for this world of ours and the human family. Yes, peace at last, the hungry fed, the homeless housed, all well clothed by a gracious distribution of the bounty God gives us all. All women and men respected a equals no matter their color, their tribe or nation, their sexual orientation. An opportunity for each to develop and use his or her God-given gifts and talents, Deep faith in a loving Father that enables us to realize and live our oneness as God's beloved children. Can we hear the aspirations of our hearts which stand in the presence of God as we pray and hear his response: Do you believe I can do this for you? And what do we answer? We live in the power of that question.

9

HOW MANY LOAVES DO
YOU HAVE?

Crowds came to Jesus, many having with them a lame
person, one maimed, one blind, a mute person and
many others. They brought them to Jesus' feet and he
healed them. So the crowd marveled seeing mutes
speak, the maimed made whole, the lame walking and
the blind seeing. And they glorified the God of Israel.
And Jesus calling up his disciples said: I am filed with
tenderness for the crowd because for three days they
have remained with me and they have nothing now to
eat. I am not willing to dismiss them without food lest
they faint on the way. And the disciples say to him:
Where in a desert place are there loaves for us, so
many as to satisfy so great a crowd? And Jesus said to
them: How many loaves do you have? And they said:
Seven, and a few little fishes. And having enjoined the
crowd to recline on the ground, he took the seven
loaves and the little fishes and giving thanks he broke
them and gave them to the disciples. And the disciples
gave them to the crowds. And all ate and were satisfied. And they gathered the leftover fragments, seven
baskets full. And those eating were four thousand men
plus women and children.

—Matthew 15:29–38

Once when I was in college I brought my class home
for supper: forty-four. Happily my Mom wasn't
phased. We rolled up the living room rug, pushed back

the furniture, and borrowed some tables while Mom cooked up an immense amount of spaghetti and my brother went out for a keg of beer. At midnight we were walking up and down the middle of the street singing. (I think that did phase Mom a bit.) It was a great party.

Jesus loved parties. Table talk seemed to be where he excelled. He was an immensely attractive and interesting talker. Crowds followed him and hung on his words. He filled the mind with astonishing new ideas—revelation, in truth—and the heart with new hope. But Jesus was a fully incarnate God. He also liked to fill the stomach with good food. Just like his Father served up the manna in the desert.

Well, this particular day, Jesus had led an immense crowd, four thousand men with their womenfolk and children, into a deserted place. He had been having almost a crusade as this crowd had been with him three days. Whatever provisions they had were gone. The food for the mind and heart he was feeding them seemed to completely distract them from bodily needs. The signs and wonders he was almost casually working fascinated them even more. People who never spoke before suddenly could speak. Twisted arms and legs were fully restored, even the cripples got up and danced and leapt for joy. And those who hadn't seen a thing for years, yes, and even those who never saw before, opened their eyes to look into the beautiful, loving, smiling eyes of Jesus. It was enough to make one forget about food.

But Jesus the perfect host did not forget. It was time for a little celebration before he brought this to a close. There was lots to celebrate in the many miraculous cures and in the rich banquet of spiritual food. Now for something to eat.

Jesus speaks so gently and so openly to his disciples:
My heart is moved. I feel tender concern for these people.
No "strong man" here, afraid to let his emotions to be
known—even feelings that we might consider belonging
to the "weaker" sex. Jesus was a man of feeling and emotion: strong "manly" emotions like anger and more gentle
ones like the pity here.

One wonders about the obtuseness of Jesus' Twelve.
Did he pick a bunch of the slowest men just so no flesh
will glory before the Lord. Jesus had been working miracles for days. And now they question as to where he is
going to get bread, how he was going to manage a feed.
This is one of the reasons why we need to keep going back
to the Sacred Scriptures in daily lectio. We too are slow to
get the full story. And as a result we have too little faith.
In actual practice we don't expect much from Jesus. We
doubt he would want to take care of our little needs, that
he would bother to. Yet he has told us that every hair on
our heads gets his particular attention. He feeds the sparrows and all the rest of the little creatures around us—
certainly he will feed us. He gives such beauty to each
flower—what color, what variety of shape and odor:
Abundance! Overflowing. And he will clothe us and make
us beautiful, too. We need to let his words and works
wash over us again and again till they seep in and transform our way of thinking and acting.

Jesus has a profound respect for us. He knows who
we are—free women and men. He knows the powers and
gifts he has given us and he expects us to use them. He
will work in our lives through them. He doesn't treat us
like babes, doing everything for us. He demands we grow
up and act like responsible adults, making our own contribution, using to the full the gifts he has given us.

How many loaves do your have? What gifts, what resources, what talents do you have to accomplish what you really want to do—what the Lord wants to do in and through you? And it isn't just a mean little thing. It is to be a party, a superabundance, with lots left over.

I would have loved to have been there and watched the apostles' faces, especially Peter who was so whole-heartedly all there in his feelings and enthusiasm. Jesus took the little they had—seven loaves and a few small fish. Leave it to fishermen to note that the fish were small. But don't we tend in the face of life's needs and challenges to judge our talents and resources as small?

Seven loaves—the Fathers of the Church and the medieval writers would have fun with the number. Peter did write: All that is written is written for our instruction. Seven is a universal number, an infinite number. However we compute our gifts, when they are allied with the power of God they are infinite in their potential. Seven here may be a foreshadowing of the seven sacraments which Jesus would give these apostles to care for the people of God—seven sacraments centered in the Eucharist, the Sacred Meal, which this miracle foreshadows. Bishops, successors of the apostolic band, have in their hands, along with the faithful in various degrees of participation, these seven "loaves"—the power to place these signs through which Jesus pours out his bounty upon us.

Jesus takes the little offering and gives thanks. Here is Jesus, God's own Son, giving thanks for such a paltry gift received through others. The power of the spirit of thanksgiving. It was through this thanksgiving—Blessed are you, Lord God of Creation, for through your goodness we have this bread—that the miracle takes place. The more we give thanks the more we will appreciate what we have and be aware of its potential in the divine power to do the impossible and more.

Yes, I would like to have been there and watched Peter. Here is a vast crowd, seated at Jesus' command, waiting in expectation for a hearty meal. As he looks out over the multitude, he looks at the half-loaf in his hand. Talk about feeling foolish! As he approached the first row of "communicants" he probably broke off little pieces hardly bigger than a communion wafer. But then he saw—no matter how much he broke off, he still had maybe even more. He broke off bigger and bigger pieces. Soon he was enthusiastically throwing pieces in all directions. Food in abundance! I dare say if we began to generously share the abundance the Lord has poured out upon this nation we would find we had even more. The Lord is the master of the sun and the rain and the fruitfulness of seed.

Have you ever had such an experience: Starting out wondering how far your meager resources would go before you ran out and then discovering that they just seemed to grow and grow and there you were, doing far more, having far more than you ever dreamed possible? I wonder if a high-school Bill Gates ever thought he would soon have more money than he could even count? Did Xavier, the student at Paris, challenged by the vision of a veteran from Spain, dare to dream of pouring the water of baptism over the head of thousands upon thousands in far off places like India and Japan? What happens in our lives is not measured by our talents, nor even by our dreams, but by our willingness to say "yes" to the Lord each day and use our gifts as he inspires and directs. Father Richard Rohr, in speaking about the New Jerusalem Community which has inspired people from all over the world, has witnessed that it wasn't something he planned or even dreamed of but something he and the community lived into day by day using what resources were at hand. And miracles happened. I experienced the same in the creation of Cistercian Publications and all that has come and is coming from that.

Jesus has a rather wry sense of humor. His boys say: We only have seven loaves. At the end of the great party he hands back to them seven full food baskets, overflowing! Get the point, boys! And we know that they don't—at least not right away. We need to sit down and take a look at our own lives, how we grew from that tiniest of organisms into the person we are today with all our weight, color and shape, as well as our gifts, talents and accomplishments. In such a context, can we doubt that we can do all things in him who strengthens us?

How many loaves do you have? Really the number is not important. He can do as much with one as with seven. We all have the gift of life, the power to love, to be there with him for others. Given that, there is nothing we can't do with him, in him, through him.

And when we are giving thanks we don't want to forget the few little fish. They may seem little indeed and we may be tempted to toss them back into the sea but they add their own flavourful dimension to the meal. I think the fish might be those very special gifts we are more inclined to call our crosses. And we are apt—like any fisherman—to see ours as actually a lot bigger than they are. When we place our sufferings objectively—and this sure is hard for us to do—along side Jesus' sufferings and the sufferings of our sisters and brothers in East Africa, Central America, or India, they are little fish. Let them be taken up in the Lord's thanksgiving, let them be used as Paul says, to fill up what is wanting in the Passion of

Christ, to make his Passion fruitfully present in the world today.

How many loaves and fish to do you have?

Take time to count them, thank God for each one, turn them over to him and courageously step forward to use them with him for the benefit of us all.

10

DO YOU SEE ANYTHING?

Jesus and his disciples arrive at Bethsaida. And some bring to him a blind man and beg Jesus to touch him. Taking hold of the blind man's hand Jesus led him forth outside the village. Spitting, Jesus with his hands applied the spittle to the man's eyes and then asked him: Do you see anything? Looking up, the blind man said: I see people, as trees, I see them walking. Then again Jesus put his hands on the blind man's eyes. Then the man looked intently and he was healed and he saw everything clearly. And Jesus sent him home, saying: Do not go into the village.

—Mark 8:22–26

A s I hear the account of the rather unusual way Jesus brought about this particular cure I get the sense that Jesus himself might have been losing patience. He had just fed a "vast crowd" with seven loaves and had seven baskets of food left over. And yet his fine friends, the Pharisees, were still carping at him, asking for a "sign from heaven." Jesus' way of using us and the little we have to work his work did not suit these proud men. They wanted manna directly from heaven. To get away from them Jesus hustled his disciples back into the boat and headed for the northern most corner of the lake. But still he was not free from exasperating incomprehension. The disciples themselves showed that they did not understand what he was trying to help them to come to realize: "Do you still not understand." I get the sense that Jesus worked this miracle slowly in stages, rather than instantaneously as he usually did, to remind himself as much as to teach us that things had to go step by step.

Our coming to see the Truth in its fullness, to see Reality, is a process. The whole of the Hebrew Bible is a story of God leading a very primitive people step by step, preparing them for the astounding revelation to be given us in the incarnate God. We are called and destined to be truly divinized, made sharers in the divine nature, life and joy. Many of the multitude of commandments or provisions that God gave his Chosen People, as he led them through the desert into a land where they could truly develop, were simple practical things for their own wellbeing: washing, not eating pork (which needed to be well-cooked, something difficult to do in the desert), sexual cleanliness and so on. One I especially like is the command from the Lord that the people carry, fastened to their belt, a small paddle on which was to be inscribed: Holy to the Lord. What was the purpose of this paddle? They were to use it to dig a hole when they needed to relieve themselves and then use it to cover things over. Holy to the Lord!

The call to divine union was indeed hinted at or even spoken of in the prophet Hosea, in the Song of Songs and elsewhere, but only in Jesus in and through the evangelical and apostolic writings is this call fully revealed. The Acts of the Apostles and the Epistles tell us of the struggle going on in the primitive Church to get hold of the sublimity of our call. And it is a struggle each one of us has in our own lives: to grasp fully that to which we are called so that it becomes a living and life-giving force in our lives.

Let us open up our "Russian doll."

This blind man was brought to Jesus by others. In one sense this is not surprising. He is blind. He needs guidance. We are all blind. We all need guidance to find Jesus. Undoubtedly there was some willingness on the part of the man to come along to Jesus. But when they arrived before the Master it was not the man himself who asked, like Bartimaeus, crying out with faith and desire. It was those who brought him who asked. Where was the man's own faith and desire? Were they weak or even absent? Or did he in his humility think it better to let others do the asking of the Master. How often people ask us monks to pray for them. Certainly the loving prayers of a friend, prayers filled with love and concern, touch the heart of God.

Curiously, these men do not ask Jesus to cure the man. They simply ask that he touch the blind man. Obviously they were looking for a cure. Perhaps their faith was like that of the women in the jostling crowd who followed Jesus en route to Jairus' house, who said to herself: If I but touch the hem of his garment I will be cured. Or maybe they did not want to put themselves out on a limb by asking directly for the miraculous. Where was their faith? Were they like the Pharisees Jesus just left, men looking for a sign or just something spectacular to excite them and give them something to talk about. They don't come across like the four who carried their friend on a mat and even climbed up on the roof and removed the roof tiles in order to bring their friend to Jesus. When Jesus saw their faith he not only healed the man lying before him but even forgave him his sins so he could make a wholly new beginning in life.

They asked Jesus to touch the man. Jesus did much more. First, he gently took the blind man by the hand and led him out of the village, away from all the curious onlookers, those wanting just the spectacle of a sign. He led him as it were away from the "world" with its values, its demands, its distractions. Away from those who had brought him to Jesus, the man now had to stand on his two feet, on his own faith and hope. It was enough to let himself be led by Jesus, led apart.

Then Jesus did what might seem very surprising to some. He spat on his hands and applied this "save" to the eyes of the man. It is such a motherly image. Can't you just see a poor mother, trying to tidy up her rag-a-muffin, using a bit of her spittle to wash some of the grim off his face and get his hair into some kind of order. Jesus was not afraid to be motherly, to speak of himself even as a mother hen who would gather her chicks beneath her wings. It is something for us, especially those of us who are clergy, but for all of us, to hear. We do no want to fail in our ministry to one another to be intimate and to reach out and touch, to be motherly and unafraid of getting our hands dirty.

We can, moreover, see here a prefiguring of baptism, the initiation that brings us enlightenment, that washes away the darkness of our sin.

Faith has begun to awaken in the man. The light has begun to dawn. He begins to see. It is a partial cure. For a blind man can we sense how exciting this was. He could now see. Light! And figures, people, and they are moving. Not clear, not distinct—something like trees, but they are walking! Could he expect more? Did his faith and hope grow with this experience? Or was he ready to settle for this. How often, when we get some little bit of spiritual insight, rather than seeing it as a divine hint of what God really wants to give us, do we settle down to munch on this crumb, satisfied, feeling good about ourselves and not eager to accept the darkness of desire that prepares us for yet greater light.

Jesus did touch this man again. And this time the healing was complete. He saw everything clearly. He could see Jesus clearly now. And there was enough faith and love there for Jesus to make yet another demand upon him: Don't go back to the village, to the "world," with its sensationalism, show, pseudo-values. Your journey, now that you have been enlightened, is to be directly to your true home.

So what do we find inside this "doll?" Our own call to leave the "world" with its values and follow Jesus. Which we can do only by grace—his hand holding ours and leading us. Our call to baptism where we receive out initial enlightenment. But as Paul reminds us, we see here only as in a mirror and an enigma. People look like trees walking. We certainly do not see the full beauty of our brothers and sisters nor even of ourselves, nor the presence of the divine within. Unfortunately, all too often we do see people as trees: alive, growing, having their springtime of beauty and their fall of decline, eventually to be cut down, good only to be burnt or remain as some dead thing in a memorial park. It is the enlightenment of faith that tells us of the spirit within and more, of the divine dimension to which every human life gives promise. We need to be touched and touched again and again, so that we might grow in insight and understanding—seeing what stands under.

Until the final touch—which comes only after the Lord has led us by the hand out of the village of this world and opens our eyes to the totally unrestricted, perfect vision of God and of ourselves and of all in God. Then we shall see even as we are seen and we shall be like him in the vision of his glory. It is promised but it is a process. For now we have to let Jesus lead us, be willing to leave the insights and values of the world and a faith that only seeks signs and wonders, be willing to accept the partial enlightenment and not give up faith and hope because of it but stay with Jesus so that he can complete the work in us.

Jesus sent the good man home. When Jesus finally fully enlightens us, then we are ready for heaven. We have a wonderful consoling teaching in the reality of a state called purgatory. Peter tells us that when the time of transition comes we will all be evaluated and even those of us who are pretty much stubble will not be rejected but we will be subjected to a fiery purification. So then, even if this process of enlightenment is not completed, even if we do find ourselves going back into the village, falling again and again into the darkness of sinful attachments and worldly desires, we can trust that the divine compassion and mercy will yet complete the healing and bring us to where we see everything clearly.

Consoling though this teaching is, nonetheless do we really want to spend our whole life groping around in semi-darkness. There is a lot of light to be found and enjoyed as we journey along. If we just stop and reflect, how significant is the light that we have already received. How different would be the whole horizon of our lives if the light of faith was absent. It is even hard to imagine. Even more difficult is it for those of us who have always lived in a world enlightened by Christian faith, albeit now a post-Christian world, to conceive of a society that has not received a glimmer of this light. We can also look back through the ages and see how humanized our world and civilization has become as the light of the Gospel permeated human consciousness directly or indirectly. Yes, we certainly have a long way to go. The very realization of that is because of the light we have already received. We have all been enlightened, some of us more, some of us less, to the extent that we have allowed the Light of Christ, through the

Gospels, through the Christian People, through the intimacy of prayer and the activity of the Spirit in the gifts, come into our lives. And there is always infinitely more. If we take time to appreciate what we have received perhaps then the desire will grow in us to open to receive more and even to actively seek it. I have often told people who were daring to set out on the way of contemplative prayer, be it by Centering Prayer or some other practice, that the first time we are brought into that experience which is literally undescribable—those who have had it have spoken of it as a "Visit of the Word," *unitas spiritus* (unity of spirit), "the kiss of the Kiss of the Mouth," and so on—our whole being says: everything that went before is worth this moment and even if it never happens again, it is all worth it. But if we continue to faithfully seek, it does happen again—again and again, until it is a very different world we live in, a very different journey. It is a journey full of light and love and peace and joy—all the fruits of the Spirit. Yes, even as a higher sensitivity and compassion allows the horrors that we perpetrate on one another in this world of ours to cut more deeply into our hearts. There yet abides in the depths of our being a joy that is beyond anything we ever conceived as possible in this life.

Yes, it is a journey. At any point we can sit by the side of the road and take our rest. We can say: it is enough for me, or: it is enough for now. The only one who puts a limit on the joy, the peace and the light which we enjoy is ourselves. Not God. God is all gift. He created only to give—to share divine happiness, which is all light, life and love. Jesus is leading each one of us. Perhaps others have first brought us to him, but as he takes us by the hand, it is our own faith and desire that open us to receiving the light he wants to give us.

11

WHERE ARE THE NINE?

As Jesus was entering a certain village, ten leprous men met him. They stood at a distance and they shouted saying: Jesus, Master, pity us. And seeing them Jesus said: Go show yourselves to the priests. And it came to pass that as they went they were cleansed. But one of them, seeing that he was cured, returned, glorifying God with a loud voice. And he fell on his face at the feet of Jesus, thanking him. He was a Samaritan. Responding, Jesus said: Were not the ten cleansed? Where are the nine? Do we find only this stranger returning to give glory to God? And Jesus said to him: Get up, go. Your faith has healed you.

—Luke 17:11–19

I wonder if the Lord is not hinting at a reality here. Do we fail nine-tenths of the time—or more—in appreciating what we are receiving from the Lord and thanking him for it. How often do we sit down and count our blessings or just think about them? And if we don't even take time to appreciate them how can we appreciate them as gifts? We will certainly fail in thankfulness.

So often it is only when we lose something that we come to appreciate it and what it has meant in our lives. Recently, through a mini-stroke, I suddenly lost the hearing in my right ear. I never before appreciated the gift of stereophonic hearing. Without two ears working it is impossible to tell from what direction a sound is coming. So when I am sharing Centering Prayer, if someone from the audience asks a question without standing up or otherwise making themselves obvious, I cannot tell from which direction the question has come. I search helplessly around the audience hoping my eyes can find some sign. Also, with one ear the background sounds blend in with those in the foreground so that if the background sounds are loud it is not possible to hear those in the foreground. This has made it impossible for me to carry on a conversation in an air plane or at a noisy dinner table or gathering. There is also the embarrassment of having someone speak to me on my deaf side and I will hear nothing. They may feel I am totally ignoring them. This is one of the reasons why I feel deafness is more of an affliction than blindness. Since it is not evident others are not aware and don't take it into account as they readily do in the case of blindness. We depend, too, on hearing to gather information from all directions while sight is limited to one.

Thanks be to our good God—in many cases he has supplied us, as it were, with a spare: two ears, two eyes, two lungs, two kidneys, two ovaries or testicles. We can loose the use of one and still manage fairly well.

In this Gospel story our Lord's outreach is to the most despised and feared of the afflicted. Again and again he reached out to these outcasts who had to keep their distance, ring their bells and cry: "Unclean." How horrible for human persons to have to publicly identify themselves as the unclean. Jesus broke through. He reached out and even touched.

We can see in the background here—within this "doll"—some of the savagery of prejudice. One of the most painful experiences I had in the course of my sojourn in India was the time I spent in a leper colony with Mother Theresa's brothers. There is, sad to say but understandably, a great bitterness and anger among these men and women exiled from human society. So much so that Mother asked the brothers to care for them because it was too dangerous for the sisters. It is estimated that fifteen percent of India is leper. This is part of the curse of prejudice. Leprosy today can be arrested in a week or two with modern medicine. But because of the prejudice victims hide their disease. Leprosy has a long incubation period—up to thirty years. And it goes through a very contagious period. So one easily infects one's whole family before the telling signs appear and one is cast out. Once the signs do appear even though the person is quickly cared for medically and no longer a threat, he or she is shunned and not allowwed to walk freely in the community because of the deep prejudice. Hence the bitterness and anger. Often lepers are reduced to the meanest state of poverty as well as being the victims of much abuse.

Add to this the fact, made clear by the evangelist, that at least this one recipient, and maybe all of them, was a Samaritan—not just a foreigner but a most despised foreigner whose very existence was considered a betrayal of ethnic solidarity and the family blood of Israel. To what can I compare a Samaritan in the eyes of Jesus' contemporaries and compatriots? A Black in southern United States in the 1960s or before, a Jew in Nazi Germany, a gay in a prestigious northeast law firm (Remember the film *Philadelphia?*), a woman executive in a businessman's world. . .? This man was doubly out of place, doubly despised as a leper and a Samaritan.

It is to such as these that Jesus reaches out. He does it because he is compassionate and loving. He does it to express his option for the poor and despised. He does it, too, to tell us that no matter how hideous our sins have made us, how unclean we are, how despised by others, we can always rely on a welcoming hearing from him. We need but cry out and he will stretch out his hand and touch us: Be thou made clean.

To cry out and receive healing we need to be conscious of our uncleanness. One of the great spiritual programs of our times is the twelve-step program of Alcoholics Anonymous, now used for many other addictions and needs. It is a basic conversion program leading all the way to wholeness, thanksgiving and outreach to others. Its foundation is faith, trust and repentance. We turn ourselves over to our Higher Power, our God of love. And we admit to ourselves, to God and to another human person that we are a helpless case. Then, with the grace of God and the support of our meeting, our group, we move ahead, cleaning up our act and entering into a way of prayer and meditation. Centering Prayer is often the choosen prayer of the eleventh-step groups.

Then there is the twelfth step—sharing with others. When we are grateful we want to share, to reach out, to tell others of the goodness of our Benefactor, to bring hope and healing and happiness to others. Cardinal Gibbons in a Thanksgiving sermon likened it to breathing. We breathe in the life-giving air to nourish our lives, going right to the heart through the bloodstream. And then we breathe out, sharing with others from the abundance of life we have received. All too many of us too much of the time come from a mentality of scarcity. We sense there is just so much and the more you get the less I get. So we compete, grab, hold on to, hoard. Look at our great stores of grain while people go hungry right in our own country not to speak of abroad. But this is because we do not know our beneficent God nor appreciate the bountifulness of his gifts. When we do we realize that the Source is inexhaustible. The more we share the more we receive. Look at the largess around us: the millions of acorns to assure the survival of the delightful and useful oak. Are we not worth more than many oaks? Look within us: the millions of semen to assure the survival of our race. Abundance beyond our comprehension.

The mentality of scarcity leads to so much of our human misery. Just on a personal level it leaves us with feelings of insecurity, of a need to compete at times to the destruction of friendship and family, leading to isolation and deep loneliness. We are plagued with unfulfilled desires that keep us from enjoying the abundance of the NOW and weigh us down with worries about the morrow. Sufficient for the day is the evil thereof. Our Lord spoke beautifully of this:

> Do not store up treasures for yourself on earth.... Be not anxious for your life, what you may eat, what you may drink; nor for your body, what you may put on. Is not the life more than the food and the body more than the clothing? Look at the birds of the heaven, they do not sow, nor reap, nor gather into barns. And your heavenly Father feeds them. Do you not surpass them? But who of you being anxious can add to his stature one inch? And concerning clothing, why are you anxious? Consider the lilies of the field, how they grow. They do not labor or spin. But I tell you, Solomon in all his glory was not clothed as one of these. If God so clothes the grass of the field which is today and tomorrow is thrown into the oven, how much more you, you of little faith? Therefore do not be anxious saying: What may we eat? Or: What may we drink? Or: What may we put on? For all these things

the nations seek after. Your heavenly Father knows
you need all these things. Seek first his kindom and
uprightness and these things shall all be given to you.
Therefore, do not be anxious about the morrow. The
morrow will be anxious for itself. Sufficient for the day
is its own evil.

Matthew 6:19, 25–34

This is the mentality of abundance. It is the mentality that comes out of appreciation and thanksgiving. It is
the mentality of confidence, peace and sharing.

It is the mentality of scarcity that is the source of
much of the violence that surrounds us: the violence of the
streets, of inner city, of white-collar crime. It is the source
of the oppression of the poor, of the cut-backs in social
spending, of immigration restrictions, of racism and ethnic oppression. It is the source of aggressive wars and of
excessively brutal response. I don't need to catalogue the
all too many recent, concrete expressions of all of this.

How different is the fruit of a spirit of thanksgiving
which flows from a mentality of abundance. As I grew up
my family passed through a period of considerable poverty.
My father, who was fortunate enough to hold a good job in
spite of the great depression of the 1930s, died very young.
My mother, who wanted only to be a homemaker, never got
much formal education and left school early to prepare for
marriage. With no credentials or experience, with the
depression still persisting, she found it very difficult to get
employment. She finally got a job working sixty hours a
week for sixty dollars a month—about ten cents an hour.
And on this we five lived. We didn't have much: oatmeal for
breakfast, peanut-butter sandwiches for lunch (Mom used
to tell us peanut butter had as much nutrition as steak and
I would think: Boy, would I prefer to have the steak! I was

so hungry that when I went to the store on Monday to get the two-day-old bread for two cents a loaf on the way home I would eat quite a few slices out of the middle hoping Mom wouldn't notice.) and potatoes for supper. I put cardboard in my holey shoes, wore my older brothers hand-me-downs which didn't work so well for we were quite different shapes, and walked a mile and three-quarters to and from school even in the first grade. Yet our home was filled with joy and gratitude. Mom used to say: We don't have much money but we have lots of fun. Thank God, there was always something to put on the table. We never went completely without a meal. And we had enough clothes albeit well-mended and patched. God was good to us. I am sure our family attitude could have been quite different and our life quite miserable. I have seen great joy and serenity in miserable-looking huts in India and East Africa and Haiti. And bickering, anger, jealousy and competition in some very affluent homes here in the United States.

Where are the nine? Each of us choosing to be the grateful one can be leaven—leavening our own homes and communities with the mentality of abundance, ensuring joy and peace and gratitude.

12

HAS NO ONE CONDEMNED YOU?

The scribes and the Pharisees brought a woman caught in adultery and standing her in the middle they said to Jesus: Teacher, this woman has been caught in the act of committing adultery. Now in our law Moses commanded that such a one should be stoned. What therefore do you say? They said this tempting him that they might have something of which to accuse him. But Jesus, stooping down, wrote with his finger on the earth. As they continued questioning him, he stood up and said to them: The sinless of you, let him cast the first stone on her. And again stooping down he wrote on the earth. And they, hearing, went out one by one beginning with the older ones. And he was left alone with the woman in the middle. And standing up, Jesus said to her: Woman, where are they? No one condemned you? And she said: No one, sir. So Jesus said: Neither do I condemn you. Go, from now on no longer sin.

—John 7:3–11

The sight was really enough to break any sensitive heart. The crude, rough mob of self-righteous men shoving, pushing, dragging the poor dishevelled woman across the square. It was bad enough that she had been used and abused by men constantly since her earliest days but now to have these arrogant, carping old Pharisees exposing her to public shame just to satisfy their own selfish, jealous ends. Finally, there she stood before the Lord, the man of unblemished purity. There was no place to hide. She and her sin stood out in the midst for all to see. Caught in adultery—she couldn't deny it. The Law said she should be stoned—who can deny it? What does the unblemished One say? Now they have him cornered.

Serenely Jesus bends over and begins to make marks in the loose sand. What was he doing? There sure has been a lot of speculation about that through the centuries.

Perhaps he was just doodling, giving them a little time to come to their senses, to reflect for a moment. Chances are though, if that were the case, most of them were too taken up with the urgency of their own agenda to give space to any useful reflection. How often in our lives does the Lord give us some time for reflection? A prolonged illness, the loss of our job, the lonely space as a primary relationship ends. How do we use the time and the space? Is it wholly taken up with self pity, bemoaning our fate? Or are we able to step back and see the graceful opportunity that hides within. The days, the weeks of forced leisure, are they a chance to examine our life and perhaps go forth from our illness with a new vision, a clearer plan, a renewed hope? Does the job loss perhaps invite us to get off the treadmill and move on to do something that we have always wanted to do, to undertake something that will give a lot more meaning and richness to our lives? Has one person walked out of our life only to make room for some other more promising relationships to grow and blossom?

Whatever be the purpose of our Lord's doodling, the conniving mob quickly enough lost patience and hurled their question at him again: The Law says stone, what do you say? At this point Jesus helped their reflection along.

No matter who we are or where we are; no matter how stupid, arrogant or conniving, the Lord never gives up on us. In one way or another he nudges us with his grace. "The sinless of you, let him cast the first stone." And he went back to his doodling. Some have speculated that Jesus might have been writing in the dust the hidden sins of these carping accusers. Or perhaps the names of other women from other times, times closer to home: Remember Judith? Remember Anna? Remember Isabel? Whatever the doodles, this time of silence, in which his challenge hung in the air, spoke eloquently. Stones hit the dust with a quiet thud. Sandaled feet thread quietly away. Yes, the oldest first. The burden of sin was heaviest upon them. And then the younger, until all had turned and departed from the scene.

There they stood, face to face—the sinner and the sinless One. "No one condemned you? Neither do I condemn you. Go, from now on no longer sin."

The first question that jumps to our minds demands attention: Where is the man? Surely he is as guilty, if not more guilty. Is he to go scot-free? Is even God a chauvinist? As horrible as the experience was for the woman, perhaps God was evening the score. She left, knowing a love and compassion which she never even dreamed existed. And a power for good. She had received a graceful invitation to change her life and the grace to do it. Whether she did or not, we do not know. It would not be easy, for how would such a one as she find a home and a way to live. Perhaps those good and for the most part nameless women who followed Jesus and provided for all his needs reached out to the hapless woman and took her into their number or at least into their care. We could expect some follow-up like that.

But the man? He probably went on his merry, sinful way. May God have mercy on his soul. But then again—great is the mercy of the Lord—maybe his salvation came through the woman. Paul tells women that they are to be the salvation of their men. Maybe the fellow was brazen enough to join the stoning crowd. Or maybe he lurked in some corner nearby, curious to see the outcome of all this. And he too saw the power and the mercy of the Master. Was it also for him a moment of grace and healing? By the mercy of God, we men sometimes get off pretty easy, certainly easier than we deserve.

On the evening of the day Jesus rose from the dead, he came into the midst of his still cowering apostles. He came to console, comfort, confirm. To bring peace. And to empower. He breathed forth his Spirit upon them. "Peace be with you. . . . Receive Holy Spirit. Whose sins you shall forgive, they are forgiven them. Whose sins you shall retain, they are retained." We Catholics see in this gift of the Risen Lord the gift of the sacrament of reconciliation, a most precious gift. How often have I had psychiatrists say to me: Oh, I wish I had your power. The Lord who made us and understands us so perfectly knows our need to hear the word of forgiveness. The patient can pour out all his sin and grief to the doctor, who in turn can speak words of compassion and assurance. But it is only the priest who can dare in God's name say: I absolve you.

But I wonder if we are not too limiting in our understanding of this gift of the Risen Lord. It is true, on another occasion when his critics ask: Who can forgive sin but God? Jesus in no way gainsaid what they said but rather affirmed his own power as God-incarnate: That you may know that the Son of Man has the power to forgive sins . . . , he went ahead and cured the young man lying before him.

Yes, only God can forgive sins. But if he has shared this power with his priests, then what would prevent his sharing it with all those baptized into his priesthood?

Our common power to forgive one another and in that forgiving bring in God's forgiveness may not be strictly of the "sacramental" order, but does that mean it is necessarily any less powerful in evoking the divine mercy.

"No one condemned you? Neither do I condemn you." This is God talking. The lack of condemnation here was rather forced and probably only external. The presence of divine mercy was extraordinary. But nonetheless the word is present and the example set. If we will forebear condemning one another, God will not condemn. Lord, make me an instrument of your pardon.

Looking at this from the other side, as it were, we can still and perhaps even more urgently pray: Lord, make me an instrument of your pardon. How important it is for us to seek reconciliation and forgiveness from any one who may be condemning us. Perhaps it is an unjust condemnation. Perhaps all the guilt lies with the other. Still there is need for reconciliation, a removal of condemnation. We are the ones who have offended God. There was surely no guilt or even the least failure on his side. Yet he came out to us to bring about reconciliation. And he says to us: Love as I have loved.

"No one condemned you?" We are Church. And how many condemn us as the Church. Our present Holy Father has gone to almost unbelievable lengths to bring about reconciliation, to lift the condemnation. One writer reports that he has apologized publicly 144 times. And as the new millennium prepares to open he courageously has led the Church into facing one of its most grievous and scandalous sins, the inquisition.

It is a reconciliation in which we can all have part. We can reach out to our Jewish sisters and brothers, to our Orthodox sisters and bothers, to our Protestant sisters and brothers, to our homosexual sisters and brothers, to our Black sisters and brothers, to all our sisters, to any who condemn us as Church and speak a word of repentance and reconciliation. We may not be able to right all the wrongs, real and not-so-real, but we can express our regret for the pain, express our heartfelt desire for complete healing, seek to be at least one Catholic who is a sign of Jesus' love and compassion in the life of this sister or brother. And out of that heartfelt concern perhaps we can pray together. More things are wrought by prayer than this world dreams of.

May the day come when we can answer the Lord as this poor adulteress: No, Lord, no one. And know the joy of hearing from him, our Judge: Neither do I condemn you.

13

WHY SHOULD IT CLUTTER
THE GROUND?

A man had a fig tree planted in his vineyard. He came
seeking fruit on it and he found none. He said to the
vinedresser: Behold, for three years I come seeking
fruit on this fig tree and I find none. Cut it down. Why
should it clutter the ground? But the vinedresser
responding, says to him: Lord, leave it also this year so
that I may dig around and manure it to see if it will
give fruit. If not, you should cut it down.

—Luke 13:6–9

Why should it clutter the ground—the limited space
on this planet of ours? It is a question we hear asked
today about a foetus, an unborn child, who promises to
come forth with downs syndrome or spondylosis or some
other deformity. Some even ask it of the child who has
already been born into life and is making his or her
painful way along life's journey, undeniably a real burden
to others. Even more persistently do we hear it in regard
to the old, especially of the victims of Alzheimer's. Ahead
there is only years of total care, without the persons' having any ability to appreciate what is being done for them.
Why should they clutter the ground?

As I mentioned before my niece and her family were
blessed with a child who had some severe neurological
problem. Thank God, some very delicate brain surgery
when he was twelve relieved Jimmy of many of the most

painful consequences of his affliction. Through the years I watched that family grow. His two older brothers, especially the oldest, and his older sister grew to be most loving, caring young people. It would be impossible to truly estimate the fullness of the gift that Jimmy gave to each one of them by being who he is.

Love is what life is about. We have always spoken of the Cistercian life as a school of love. But every life is or is meant to be a school of life.

The wonderful little story Jesus tells here begins with years of fruitlessness. It goes on to speak of being spaded and dug about and poked at and then manured. Distasteful stuff, earthy stuff. Sometimes a lot of human manure has to be literally taken care of. All our lives are in some ways manured. My confrere, Father Vincent Dwyer, likes to draw an image from his boyhood. On their farm in the cowbarn there was a trap door in the middle of the floor. All the manure was shovelled through this trap door to fall into a cart below. Vince said growing up he felt he was standing under that trap door and people were forever shovelling manure on top of him. I think many of us feel that way at times. We can draw some hope and consolation from our Lord's words here.

In today's world hardly a person is not touched by the demands that family afflictions place upon us. In medieval times monks built houses just outside the monastery gate where they could receive their parents and care for them in their old age. Today, more than one monk and nun has had to leave the cloister and go home to care for an aging parent. One of our brothers was home for seven years, another for over a dozen. One can hardly imagine a more complete disruption of a life than this. Yet in responding to this filial duty these men grew in love. And isn't that the reason why they came to the monastery in the first place, why the Lord invited them, so that they might grow in love.

Marriage, too, is surely a school of love. We need to remember that there are two kinds of love. There is the love of enjoyment, of pleasure, when there is freedom to enjoy the presence of the beloved. And there is the love of desire when we are deprived of that enjoyment. We all want the maximum of freedom to enjoy those whom we love. It is most important that we do get some time regularly to do this. There are emergencies when we are called to unrelenting giving and serving but such sinuations should not be allowed to last to the breaking point. We need to know how to get help and when to ask for it. We want to get the support we need and give others the opportunity to help—our family, our friends, our parish, the others who are there to support and help.

The times that are filled more with the love of desire, of longing are important for us. This is where our love most grows. This love prepares us so that when the time comes we can find greater enjoyment in the experience of our loved ones, a greater quality in our relationships. It is important that we see our self-giving love in this way. Sacrifice in love, yes, but it looks to the promise. If we give ourselves over to resentment in the midst of the demands placed upon us, our hearts will be poisoned; there will be no possibility of our finding joy in love when the time of freedom comes for that. A martyr complex only makes our self love grow and undermines our ability to give ourselves into the joy of love.

We all know of Mother Teresa, admire her and applaud her being honored with the Nobel Prize. She deserves it and much more. I could tell you many stories about Mother but let me just share this one.

Mother was in some ways a very tough and demanding woman. She made great demands on her novices. She
did not want any woman to make profession in her community until they knew, not just in theory but in the fabric of their being, that it is a privilege to serve Christ in all
his appearances and above all in the poorest and most
wretched. In Mother's communities several hours are
allotted to prayer at the beginning of the day. But to help
the second year novices to grow into this realization, they
had a special program.

In India the train stations are public dormitories. At
night they are covered, wall-to-wall, with sleeping bodies.
Indians in general are very compassionate and caring
people. But they have great difficulty in three particular
cases. A malformed or handicapped child is often dis-
carded. This is why Mother established her creches wherever she could. Then there are the lepers. These are seen
as cursed by God and are cast out. For these often very
angry persons, Mother supported her brothers in estab-
lishing colonies where they can live in peace and earn a
living. Finally there is the old person who is slowly dying.
The family solution is often to take such persons to the
train station and bed them down with all the others.
When the well arise in the morning they remain there till
they die and are taken away by the sweepers to be burned
at the ghats. It is to these poor abandoned ones that
Mother directed the love of her novices.

After an hour of prayer, the second-year novices would
go out—and often Mother would go with them—to gather
up those left in the stations and bring them to the sisters'
home for the dying. Here they would minister to them and
do all they could to help these dear ones die with dignity.

One morning Mother went out with the novices. When they arrived back at the home they had a particularly wretched case. The poor man had been gnawed by rats. Maggots had also eaten away his flesh in places, right down to the bone. There wasn't much left of him. Mother said: I will take care of this dear one. For much of an hour Mother did all she could to clean the man and make him comfortable. Finally, as she was again soothing his face with a cool cloth, he opened his eyes and said: Thank you. And with that he died. Mother rose and went to his feet and prostrated full length. Later that day when I met Mother she said to me, with a beaming face: This morning I had the privilege of caring for the dying Christ.

For us Christians certainly this is part of the mystery: seeing Christ in these least ones, these most needy ones: Whatever you do for the least of mine, you do for me. I was sick and you cared for me. Seeing Christ and rejoicing that we have this opportunity to care for him who cared enough for us so as to live and die for us—this is the realization Mother Teresa wanted for all her sisters. To come to this level of realization and joy we must cultivate our love of Jesus. We need to get to know him more and more through meeting him in Scripture and prayer.

Love enables us to enjoy caring for others. I remember one day watching my sister-in-law changing her infant's diaper. For many this would be a distasteful task. I know it would be for me. Yet Pat was undoubtedly having a wonderful time. And she took her time. She must have taken all of twenty minutes or half an hour. The communication of love pouring out upon that child—what a sacrament of God's love for us. And there could be no doubt this woman was happy in her love.

Such loving care is not easy when it goes on year after year, with no sign of let up. All the more so when the recipient seems less and less capable of appreciating what is being done for him or her. And yet, except in the most extreme cases, our very presence, the touch of love, does bring some sense of comfort, some pleasure to the loved one, maybe more than we realize.

Why then clutter the human scene with these poor wrecks? Because human life is about love. And they offer us, with proper response, a great opportunity to grow in love. Certainly it is a happier situation when we can minister in love, be there in love to loved ones who are not afflicted: to the joyful, healthy child; to the comfortable, content parent who is aging beautifully. But we have to admit that not only is there not so much of a challenge here, but in fact we often neglect to offer caring love to the one whose affliction is not demanding. I doubt my great nephews and niece would have ever learned to be such loving brothers and sister if Jimmy had not been afflicted.

But now let us open our little Russian doll and look inside. Why is this so: that in many cases attention only comes when we are challenged by affliction? Looking at this question may give us an opportunity to take a better look at ourselves, to clean house a bit. For there is probably a bit of a mixed bag here.

For one thing, my sense of my own inadequacy is not challenged in the face of one afflicted. Indeed, I can sense a certain superiority, an ability to supply. The jealousies, the competitiveness, the sibling rivalry that eat into so much of my relating loses much of their base. I have more freedom for my innate goodness to surface. Maybe, just maybe I will get in touch with how really good I am in spite of the overlay that I have allowed a sinful climate to teach me to develop. The reality is, by the goodness of God, I do have many wonderful gifts which I most commonly simply take for granted. All that I have is gift. As I see the one afflicted I can well say, there, but for the grace of God, go I.

This question invites us to look at our other relationships: with our siblings who are not so afflicted, with our parents who are not yet so needy. It can invite us to begin to expend more self-giving love to building them up, doing what we can to make their lives fuller, richer, happier. Indeed it can fill our hearts with gratitude for the well-being of our children, our parents, all our loved ones—our own well being.

I have said it myself at times. I heard my mother say it many times. And I have heard many others say it: I do not want to be a burden to others. The more we have found the caring for others, especially our loved ones, a painful burden, the more is such a sentiment apt to take over in our lives.

Among my friends I had a wonderful Jewish family. The only son was a Yale graduate, a very successful young lawyer. Then one day came the dread news: AIDS. Steve was dead within two years. It was indeed a long painful two years, watching him waste away, with all his gifts and talents. Not very long after his cremation, his mother was suddenly diagnosed with pancreatic cancer. It took the disease only a few months to complete its life-destructive work. That Thanksgiving, dad went up to New York to join his family. At dinner he thanked them all for all they had done for him and his family. Then he went into his room and put a revolver in his mouth. That bullet left a big hole in all our hearts.

Can I be a gift of God to others in my need? Is that why he lets me linger on with increasing dependancy. Do they have a need for me to be here to give them a chance to learn more about self-giving love? As long as I am able, can not my smiles, my affirmation, my expressed gratitude help them to get a little more in touch with their innate goodness?

For me dependancy can be a school of humility, a basic human virtue, a doorway to reality. As I experience a new and growing dependence I am invited to realize more my total dependence on God and others as the agents of God. I was totally dependent for years as an infant. And dependance has been part of my whole life in many ways: my need for air, for food, for shelter, for clothing, for moral support, for friendship, for intellectual and emotional stimulation. . . . Sad to say, it is often only when we lose some of these things that we begin to really appreciate the gift we have taken for granted perhaps for decades. But we can also learn from the loses of others if we are attentive and compassionate.

These needy ones do not clutter the ground. They are there for us. They invite us to appreciate and they invite us to grow. They invite us to be more generous. To reach out in love even further then we thought we could. One of the images that remains strongly in my memory is that of the Pope standing in a blustery rain at the foot of Wall Street in New York and telling us affluent Americans that we need to give more, give not just from our surplus but even from our substance.

I am abundantly cared for. Do I care for others, for Christ in others? Yesterday I received a mailing from Food for the Poor. Ferdy Mahfood, the founder of this outreach, in a very personal letter tells me he can build a home for a homeless family in Haiti for only $1,000. Certainly anyone who can afford two homes (or more) can certainly afford a third for the needy and send Ferdy a $1,000 each year for his home-building project. Indeed, many with only one home can still afford this gift to a family in need. I keep now on my desk the picture Ferdy sent of the shacks in which these families now live—if such shelters can even be called shacks—and I pray that the Lord will stretch many hearts to give even out of their substance and provide a home for the homeless Christ.

The fact is, our affluence, rather than freeing us to enjoy life and love more, often begins to make great demands upon us and fill us with fear and concern. We watch the stock market as it veers up and down. My brother has his computer so programmed that that is the first thing that comes up when he turns it on. Happily, he is a man who goes each day to Mass with his wife and receives the Word of God so he keeps things in perspective and lives with a generous and free spirit. But that is hardly true of many stock-market watchers. Without a sense of Divine Providence and the gratitude and generosity that flows from that, what should be bearing the fruit of freedom to enjoy life can rather burden it with clutter.

In our down times, I think we all find ourselves asking: why do I clutter the ground? Yes, to give others a chance to grow in love. But as the caretaker in Jesus' parable sensed, there is still promise in the future. We need fallow times. In the all-wise legislation of the Divine in the Hebrew Bible, the Lord provided for the jubilee years, years when the earth was allowed to lie fallow. We here-and-now people don't like this very much. We find the "dark nights," the down times very difficult. If we can get hold of the value of this, like the good farmers of old (who did use manure instead of forcing the soil constantly with artificial chemicals, leading to we know-not-what future disaster), we will be able to accept with more peace and live in hope and expectation. We can let the creative juices flow, let in the new open spaces that the digging brings, the enriching juices of the manure, a deeper humility with its freedom. We can come to realize hidden potential, frustrated potential and in that realization know new joy!

14

DID YOU NOT KNOW?

Completing the days of the feast, when it came time to return, the boy Jesus remained in Jerusalem and his parents knew it not. Supposing him to be in the company, they went a day's journey. Then they sought him among their relatives and acquaintances. Not finding him, they returned to Jerusalem seeking him. And it came to pass that after three days they found him in the Temple sitting in the midst of the teachers, hearing them and questioning them. All hearing him were astonished at his intelligence and his answers. Seeing him, his parents were astonished. And his mother said to him: Child, why did you do this to us? Your father and I are greatly distressed seeking you. And he said to them: Why is it that you sought me? Did you not know that I must be about my Father's business? And they did not understand the word he spoke to them.

—Luke 7:43–50

It is interesting that the first recorded words of both Jesus and Mary are questions. And it is question from Mary, his mother, that calls forth Jesus' first question.

Mary's first question is a primary question for all of us: "How will this be . . . ?" How is God's will, God's plan, to be accomplished in our lives. Of course, it presupposes that we have made some sure discernment in regards to what that will might be. In this regard Mary seems to get off easy. She has a divine messenger who comes to her and makes known to her just what God wants. But actually it wasn't as easy as all that. Mary had already gone through what must have been a long, soul-searching process to come to the decision to live a virginal life and to marry Joseph as the virginal protector of that virginity. It was only because she had made this discernment and held it with a certain sureness that her question now arises. Otherwise, the question of an engaged woman becoming a mother would not be a question. God's plans for us as we discern them may not be so contradictory. But if we want to fulfill them with sureness we need to constantly ask in prayer: How will this be? How am I to bring this about in my life? Or how am I to collaborate as God brings this about in my life? We need to live in this question, among others.

Like Mary, we want it to be for us a question full of faith, and not like the question of her elderly cousin who questioned because he doubted. We ask with confidence, knowing that the loving will of God can and will be accomplished in us and in our lives, seeking only to know the way in so far as we need to live into a complete "yes" as Mary so well exemplifies for us.

And yet the answer will not always be clear for us. And even when it is clear, the working out of it will have its problems and fears. The angel made it clear to Mary how she was to conceive as a virgin: Holy Spirit would overshadow her. But that didn't clear up the matter with Joseph, her betrothed, or anyone else for that matter. Filled with faith and love as she was, there was still room for fears and questioning in Mary's heart as she set out across country to her cousin's.

What is perhaps more meaningful for us is the scene where Mary calls forth her Son's first reported words, his question. How human, how motherly is this revelation of

Mary, the sinless one. With all the pathos of a good Jewish mother she doesn't hesitate to remonstrate: "Why have you done this to us?" Even across the ages the pain is so poignant that we can feel it in our bones. We can just begin to imagine all the thoughts and fears that raced through Mary's mind and heart as she and Joseph searched for their Child.

Sometimes our pain is too deep, too all-encompassing to leave room for any logical answer, or even for a word of faith. I have a priest friend who is outstanding for his compassion. He is known by all as a man who can be there for you no matter what. In recognition of this the bishop put him in charge of the ministry to the divorced and remarried and of the ministry to God's gay and lesbian sons and daughters. And then he appointed him spiritual father at the seminary—a role model as well as a companion and friend for all the future priests of the diocese. Not long after he was asked to be spiritual father at the seminary in Rome. I once asked Father how he had come to be such a compassionate listener. In reply he told me the story of his first night on duty as a priest.

He had been ordained two weeks before and had come to his first parish the previous Friday. It was now Tuesday evening and he was alone in the rectory, his first night "on duty." A call came from the hospital. There had been an accident. Four teenagers had crashed into and over a guard rail. The bodies were being brought into the emergency room. When Father arrived the medical personnel were busy, efficiently going about their sad duty. The police seemed to have everything under control. Everybody seemed to know just what he or she was supposed to do except the newly ordained. He stood there feeling very helpless and useless. Suddenly there was a great commotion at the door. The parents of three of the victims had arrived. The police chief caught Father's arm; "That's your job." And the chief and his officers hustled the parents and the priest into a side room. A very belligerent father was shouting: "Where is my son? I have a right to see my son." He all but knocked Father over as he pushed him aside. Father sought to restrain him. And he shouted all the more: "Why can't I see my son?" Father blurted it out: "Because he is dead. They are all dead." The four parents collapsed on the couch in stunned shock and then burst into tears. Father fell into a chair opposite them, held hands and wept with them. He didn't know what to say. He knew there was nothing to say.

When he finally got back to the rectory that night, Father lay sleepless, feeling a complete failure. Everybody else seemed to know exactly what they should do. All he could do was blurt out the horrible news and cry. Morning was long in coming.

When it did come and passed on to afternoon, Father received a phone call from the undertaker in the next town. Would he be willing to come over and conduct the vigil service the next evening. The parents requested it. The particular lad did not belong to his parish but he could hardly refuse. Another first for Father.

As he edged his way through the crowd towards the coffin, he became painfully aware of the fact that people were pointing at him and making some comment to their neighbors. Everybody knew what a failure he was. He got through the service as best he could and made his way toward the door. The parents and an uncle followed after. When they reached the vestibule the uncle asked Father if he would be willing to conduct the funeral the next morning. It was the parents' request. Father was taken aback.

The uncle went on to say: "They have told everyone how you were with them. You didn't try to offer any hollow-sounding words but just sat and wept with them in their great grief." It was a moment of enlightenment for Father. It is by being broken and in tears that we can best be with those who are broken and in tears.

Some sorrows are too deep for words. It is a time to be with and be with in silence. There are human sorrows. Recently friends lost a son on the eve of his high school graduation. Danny and Katie did not want words, no matter how full of faith; they just wanted us to be with them in love and pain. And there is another searing pain for the faithful, the sense of being abandoned and even betrayed by God. With Jesus on the cross the cry rises up from the depths: My God, my God, why have you forsaken me? Deprived of the "being with," even the "being with" of God—who can endure it.

Mary not only lost a Son; she lost her God who had entrusted himself to her as a Son. When she found him, as fit as ever and so at peace, all the pent-up emotion of the days of anguished searching broke forth: "Why did you do this to us?" As much as we feel for the mother, how good it is for us to hear this sinless one give vent to her frustration and anger, her incomprehension. It is all right at appropriate times to be very angry with God. And to give vent to that anger in a prayer that shakes its fist and asks indignantly: Why? Or to give voice to a deep pain, to true anguish: Why? why? why? Or to the utter mystery of it all, the incomprehension: Why?

But Jesus' response was not one of compassionate silence, at least not at this time. Perhaps there was a lot of compassion in his tone and demeanor. We do not know. Certainly his question can come to us in a very accusing way: "Did you not know . . . ?" "Where's your faith? You shouldn't have been worrying. You should have known." But I would rather hear here a compassionate tone. In our darkness, in our questioning, he is here, if only we have the ears of faith to hear: "Do you not know . . . . ?" It is the answer that Revelation gives us, in the very mouth of the Word, to which our faith needs to rise. We can be consoled by the fact that even the Blest Virgin did not understand. Often we will not understand. But faithful one that she was, she pondered his words in her heart. And the invitation to do the same is ours.

If we look through some of the many English translations of the New Testament, we will find that the words of the Lord here have given birth to two distinct interpretations. Perhaps the more favored one is: "Did you not know that I must be about my Father's affairs?" or "my Father's business?" Indeed this is the answer, albeit a question, to all the doings of the Lord in our regard. And often enough our answer to his question has to be an honest "no." We often do not know that it is he about his Father's business and that is why we suffer so much more than we need to. We do not know. We know only the pain, the absence, the loss, the sorrow, the conflict, the contradiction. Yes, Paul did say: "For those who love God, all things work together unto good." It is God working. Often God working anonymously through the occasions of life, the daily happenings, the circumstances of every day, the vicissitudes of nature, even the freedom of poor, weak sinful men and women and even that of the malicious, if there be any. The Son is about his Father's business, the prime affair of this whole creation, after the glory of God and in which that glory most especially resides: in the sanctification of his saints.

Sometimes this is the last thing we can hear. And the last thing we want to hear. We have our image of God. For the most part it is a benign God. We work hard at suppressing the dark side of God (if I can say that without being guilty of blasphemy), at least those of us who are trying to enter into a closer union with God in Christ. But how can we reconcile some things with a benign God, even if ultimately they do work together for our good? Not to speak of the horrors that can sometimes be and often are traceable to the sinful use of our freedom, like teenagers—or innocent bystanders—being killed by drunken driving, or AIDS, or lung cancer caused by smoking. What of tornadoes, volcanoes, hurricanes and typhoons? What of malaria, typhoid, cancer, and epilepsy? What of birth defects, blindness, deafness, and down's syndrome? How the innocent suffer! A benign God? About his Father's business? Some questions we have to live with. As wise old Job in the end perceived, for us on the journey there is no answer—yet. As God told us through his prophet Isaiah: "My thoughts are not your thoughts, nor my ways your ways, but as high as the earth is above the heavens so are my thoughts beyond your thoughts and my ways beyond your ways." We do not have the answer. We do have the challenge. We can live in the question and enter ever more deeply into the mystery of God. Somehow it is a mystery of love. It challenges us. And somehow, too, if we let the words gently re-echo within, they do bring a great comfort: "Do you not know I must be about my Father's business?"

Must? Yes, the love of Christ compels. It compels him, his love for us. It compelled him to come to earth, to enter our human family; it compelled him all the way to the cross. He must be about his Father's business because he loves the Father and does always the things that

please the Father. He must be about his Father's business because he loves us and his Father's business is our
salvation and sanctification, our full participation in his
unending joy.

Why does it have to be done this way? Augustine once
said in regard to another question (The reconciliation of
God's foreknowledge and our free will.): If you don't want
to be wrong, don't ask. That word applies equally well
here. If we, who are made in the image of God, have our
freedom, how much more so God? Still, what seems to be
cruelty, how do we reconcile it with the divine benignity?
We live with the question. And enter more deeply into the
divine mystery.

The other common interpretation of this word of the
Lord is not so challenging: "Did you not know that I must
be in my Father's house?" And where is that house for us
today now that the temple of Jerusalem lies in ruins. "The
Father and I will come and we will make our home in you."
In times of intense suffering and pain, when we have been
terribly wronged, when we are to all intents and purposes
abandoned by God himself, who can hear the word of
faith? Hear it loud enough, clear enough for it to be consoling? It is true. God is here within. We are never truly
abandoned. Never truly left alone. If we can rise to the
occasion and enter within, we can perhaps know a great
consoling. Such a friendship, such a love is ours.

This, of course, brings us to something dear to my
heart: Centering Prayer. Here, for fifty years and more, in
the darkest of times as well as in the bright, I have found
my consolation and strength. I will speak briefly of this
ancient form of Christian meditation in an appendix. For
now, let me say, it is simply accepting this word of faith
and responding to it. Yes, I know you must be in your

Father's house. And I accept your invitation: "Come to me all you who labor and are heavily burdened, and I will refresh you." Even when I am burdened with burning questions in the midst of searing pain, I know, I believe that he is at home in me and I can come to him.

Do you not know that I must be in my Father's house? Yes, Lord, I know? And if I cannot always rejoice in that presence, I can rest in it and find refreshment for my soul. And often enough for my body, also.

15

WHO IS MY MOTHER AND WHO ARE MY BROTHERS?

While Jesus was still speaking his mother and brothers stood outside seeking to speak with him. And
someone said to him: Behold, your mother and your
brothers are standing outside seeking to speak to you.
And answering, he said to the one who told him: Who
is my mother and who are my brothers? And stretching forth his hand to his disciples he said: Behold my
mother and my brothers. For whoever does the will of
my Father in the heavens, that one is my brother and
sister and mother.

—Matthew 12:46–50

Who is my mother and who are my brothers? This time
Jesus answers his question himself. At least he gives
one answer—the dimension he wants to teach at this
moment. And it is wonderful: Whoever does the will of my
Father in the heavens, that one is my brother and sister
and mother. Jesus is bringing forth a wonderful exciting
reality.

Jesus is, of course, the Man from Nazareth and Mary
is his Mom. She did for him everything a Mom does. What
were those days when he was being formed in her womb?
There was fear, yes, until the angel straightened things
out with Joseph. (Why do we always think of the negative
first?) Only a mother can really enter into the joy, hopes,
fear and pain of Mary's pregnancy, the joy of her sharing

with her cousin Elizabeth, the wonder of that night when she first held her Child in her arms and felt him suck at her breast. Jesus, the God who commanded us all to honor our mothers, could not fail to honor his. And here he is paying her high honor setting her up as the model for the way we are to foster the gestation and growth of the whole Christ, the fullness of who he is in his creation. Pondering on Mary and on all the dimensions of her motherly life, just as she pondered in her heart on all her experiences, gives us great insight as to how we are to live. Mary's seven words recorded in the Gospels form a whole rule of Christian life. But as we all, she teaches or models more by the way she lives than by what she says.

One thing is eminently clear. It is by doing the will of the Father that we are Christ's mother, that we mother the Christ in ourselves and in one another. Whether it is by sitting at the feet of Jesus as that other Mary or by bustling about like her sister—it is by doing what God wants of us that we make our contribution to the central undertaking of the creation: the forming of the whole Christ.

It is good to recall that most of what Mary did was everyday stuff. Indeed she was so conscious of the fact that this was her vocation: to simply be the mother of Jesus, God though he was, that she didn't hesitate to scold and even needed a reminder that there was another dimension to her Child that she had to respect to let it call forth its own actions.

It must have been a sorrowful day for the widow of Nazareth when her only Son, a model of love and care, said his good-bye and set out on the pastoral dimension of his mission. Losing Jesus in some way, seeking him and being apparently rebuffed, as is Mary here, having the years of special faithful motherly service go unacknowledged, is part of our mothering the whole Christ. After very consoling periods of special intimacy with God there come the periods when we seem to be lost in the crowd, only able to see him from afar. Yet we can be sure, if we are faithful in seeking to be with him and do follow as best we can, in the end we will be brought into a most intimate sharing in his saving death. And this will be as painful as it will be consoling. And it will lead to resurrection and ascension.

The questions that Jesus addressed to his mother, the "Why did you seek me?" in the Temple and the "What's it to us?" at Cana, along with this question, can seem very hurtful for Mary. But each of them, we see as we reflect upon them, leads to a higher level of understanding of Mary and her relation with her Son and his mission. We may at times find the questions of the Lord, the questions of life, very threatening and painful, but we want to follow them through and they will bring us to a higher and fuller level of understanding.

As I said above, only a mother can really enter into the experiences that were Mary's in her pregnancy and indeed in the rest of her mothering. Also I think it is only a mother who can really understand what Jesus is saying here when he says we mother him by doing the Father's will. It tells us something of what we might expcet the Father's will to demand of us. It tells of the nurturing care we should bring to the Christ being formed right now, yes, in the universal Church, in the whole of the human family but more significantly for each one of us, in our own home, in our own family, in our own community. A mothering attitude—in the best sense of that reality—is what each one of us, even us macho men, want to bring. I must confess it is not an easy thing to do in a community of male celibates. We men are so competitive and naturally combative. Doesn't the men's movement urge us to be warriors and kings? Certainly not mothers! It is a real challenge to seek to be so integral—to be motherly even while we are brotherly, real men to real men and real women. It can be of some consolation to us, perhaps, if we can see some of the cares and concerns we do find invading our lives, some of the pains, as generative, as a part of our participation in the gestation of the whole Christ.

Mary has much to teach us. A lifetime of walking close to her, for over six decades now, finds me feeling there is still so much to learn from Mother Mary—to learn to integrate into my life.

Again, the superabundance of the revelation comes to us in an almost paradoxical call: to be mothers and to be brothers and sisters. There is some connatural space here for us men. We know by experience what it means to be brother. Even if we haven't a blood brother, dimensions of the natural bond usually find their place in our lives. But again we have to look to our sisters and do some real open listening and observing to get at least some insight into what it means to be sisters to the Lord. I was listening to Richard Rohr yesterday—a talk he was giving to one of our Trappist communities. Richard was sharing what it has meant in his life as a Friar to move out of the friary and live in a mixed community. He confessed he was often tempted to flee back to the friary. As he put it: many an evening he and sister ended up shouting at each other as they did the dishes. But he celebrated and rejoiced in all he had learned about being a sister as well as a brother of Christ. I wonder if it wouldn't open up some wonderful new dimensions to the marital relationship if the husband came to it with a conviction that he had a lot to learn from his wife about being a mother and sister to Christ in his fellows.

Who is my mother and who are my brothers? I hope I am, Lord. I want to be, you know that. I want to be—at least in theory. But I have to admit that the very thought of acting feminine in any way, of taking on any of what we call "feminine characteristics," scares me so deeply that it makes my stomach cramp. From the earliest taunts of the school yard, "sissy" has been a most dreaded label and libel. Above all we have to be men, masculine through and through. It takes a lot to let this go in the realization that a fuller actualization of our humanity lies in integrating in an appropriate way those characteristics we call "feminine." Putting it all together is a challenge. I don't think we have to figure it all out in our heads *a priori*. Rather we have to dare to be open, to learn from our sisters and to put what we learn into practice, things like letting our emotions be there and surface and be expressed, speaking the kind and loving word, making the kind and gentle gesture, being sensitive persons. Welcoming into our lives beauty of all sorts: poetry, music, flowers, decor. That doesn't fit too readily into the image we have of ourselves as men. We don't want to be seen as effeminate—and certainly we do not want to be effeminate. Integrating the human values and virtues we have too specifically labelled "feminine" does not equal effeminacy. If I may say it, we need to make these ours in a masculine way.

We may fear even more being thought to be a "homo," a faggot. It is a sad and rather odd conception of things that we end up putting together in our minds and values those who have integrated the "feminine" dimension of the human person and a group of our brothers who are all too often despised and looked down upon. Maybe if we find the freedom to break away from the filters of a narrow male image we might be able to let go of some of the defensive prejudices we habor in regard to our gay brothers. Their response brought out into the open by the AIDS pandemic asks us if they perhaps are not generally doing a better job of mothering Christ in their fellows than their "hetero" brothers.

I certainly have been writing this chapter from the male perspective. (I was tempted to say: Well, what can you expect from a male. But then all I have been saying hit me right between the eyes. Maybe you have a right to expect more. I am still a learner. After all I am only 67!) I suspect it is in the depths just as challenging for a woman to integrate the "masculine virtues" into her response and thus be brothers to Christ. But I feel very much out of my own depth to attempt to address this. I will only say I think our sisters have a bit of a head start here in this call to be fully integral humans in living out our particular vocations and thus mothering, sistering and brothering the whole Christ.

The will of God for each one of us is a fully integral humanity, open to complete invasion by and union with the divine. It is lived out in the many little acts that make up our day as we walk in the path of our own particular vocation. And Jesus in his question invites us to realize that the many seemingly little ordinary everyday kindnesses and fidelities are actually part of a sublime vocation, one like unto that of Mary, the holy Mother of the God-Man. The more I can get hold of this wondrous reality the happier and more meaningful my life is going to be even when on the surface it seems to be a terribly ordinary existence doing terribly ordinary things over and over and over. The challenge is to bring to all this the insight of faith and to seek to do it in an ever more integral way.

A CONCLUDING WORD

I started to entitle this brief chapter "A Final Word" but there is nothing final about it. Indeed, as I hand this manuscript over to my publisher I feel very incomplete. Our Russian doll stands there to be opened again and again and again. There is so much more to be found living in these questions. We have only begun to open them out. And these are only fifteen of the questions asked by Jesus. There are so many, many more. And there are all the questions that were asked of Jesus. And then there are all the questions that arise from these questions as we begin to hear the answers.

We need time.

Time for prayer. No one knows the Son but the Father and those to whom the Father reveals him. Jesus told Peter frankly when the blundering apostle rose to his magnificent declaration: Flesh and blood did not reveal this to you. It was my Father in the heavens. (And no one knows the Father but the Son and those to whom he reveals him.)

We need time to let Jesus and his friends tell us his story. And then let that story interface with our own story. Here is where life is: in the story. A run-away best seller in 1997 was *Angela's Ashes,* the frank, hearty story that a witty Irishman had the courage to tell about his struggle to rise from an impoverished youth, impoverished in many ways. Thomas Merton's *Seven Storey Mountain,* which once sold ten thousand copies in a single day, still speaks to thousands and thousands each year— fifty years later. The honest story, it speaks to our heart— if we let it. We need to let the story of Jesus speak to our hearts. This is precisely why Jesus came down from heaven and, just like the rest of us, lived for nine months in a womb, grew at a mother's breast, played in the street, studied his alphabet, learned a lot about being a man from his father. He had to eat and sleep and bathe; he sweated like the rest of us. He laughed, he sang, he cried, he danced, he knew what it was to be tired at the end of a day's labor. Yes, he knew fear and pain and loneliness and heart-breaking disappointment. And he cried. He wanted in every way to share our story so we could share his. For he prayed, he spoke intimately to God and of God, his Father. He knew, in a way he wants us to know, that God is our Father. (Father for in no way excluded any of the wonderful qualities of Mother.) His story and his stories are all about this. His constantly recurring questions are open doors inviting us into the sharing of this.

We want to let his story speak to our hopes and to our fears, to carry us beyond them, to a realm of light and love and peace and joy—a joyful peace that comes from knowing we are held in a most caring love. Are you not worth more than many sparrows? Look how he feeds the birds of the air, clothes the lilies of the field. If poor sinful fathers are responsive to their child's needs, how much more so the heavenly Father.

There is a story coming from war-scarred Europe that speaks to me as a kid who grew up in the depression and was always hungry. After the hostilities ceased, there was a multitude of parentless children wandering around the empty battle fields. They were gathered into orphanages. Though they were well enough cared for in these orphanages, they still had a hard time settling down and sleeping at night. Then a psychiatrist who had attentively listened to the children's stories got an inspiration. Each child was given a large loaf of bread, not to eat but to sleep with. They were to get all they wanted to eat at supper but they would have this big loaf to take to bed. Almost immediately the children began to sleep peacefully. They just needed this tangible bit of evidence that they would be taken care of tomorrow.

Paul tells us that peace is one of the fruits of the Spirit—the Spirit who is the Father's and Jesus' love dwelling in us, bringing us into the experience of that love, enabling us to truly enter into the story of this Son. Not once but twice the heavens opened and the Father spoke in our hearing: This is my beloved Son, my chosen One. Listen to him. Listen to his story. We need this daily bread for the soul.

And if we really open to this story, it will not only give us the peace that comes from the security of caring love. It will bring to our lives the sparkle that comes from promise and expectation. We are the guests at the wedding feast, peeking through the curtains, waiting for the blushing groom to arrive. We are the servant to whom much has been entrusted and we are waiting for the Master to return so we can show him what we have done with what he has given us. Eye has not seen, ear has not heard, nor has it even entered into the human imagination what God has prepared for us, but the Spirit through these stories gives us some intimation of what is to come. It is exciting to live in the question.

Some Additions

THE QUESTIONS OF JESUS

The Gospel of Saint Matthew

Mt 5:13	But if the salt loses its taste, with what can it be seasoned?
Mt 5:17	Do you think I have come to abolish the law and the prophets?
Mt 5:46	For if you love those who love you, what recompense will you have? Do not the tax collectors do the same?
Mt 5:47	And if you greet your brothers and sisters only, what is unusual about that? Do not the pagans do the same?
Mt 6:25	Is not life more than food and the body more than clothing?
Mt 6:26	Are you not more important than they [the birds in the sky]?
Mt 6:27	Can any of you by worrying add a single moment to your life-span?
Mt 6:28	Why are you anxious about clothes?
Mt 6:30	If God so clothes the grass of the field, which grows today and is thrown into the oven tomorrow, will he not much more provide for you, O you of little faith?
Mt 7:3	Why do you notice the splinter in your brother's eye, and do not perceive the wooden beam in your eye?
Mt 7:9f	Which one of you would hand his son a stone when he asks for a loaf of bread, or a snake when he asks for a fish?

Mt 7:16	Do people pick grapes from thornbushes, or figs from thistles?
Mt 8:26	Why are you terrified, O you of little faith?
Mt 9:4	Why do you harbor evil thoughts?
Mt 9:5	Which is easier, to say, "Your sins are forgiven," or to say, "Rise and walk?"
Mt 9:15	Can the wedding guests mourn as long as the bridegroom is with them?
Mt 9:28	Do you believe that I can do this?
Mt 10:34	Do you think that I have come to bring peace upon the earth?
Mt 11:7	What did you go out to the desert to see? A reed swayed by the wind?
Mt 11:8	Then what did you go out to see? Someone dressed in fine clothing?
Mt 11:9	Then why did you go out? To see a prophet?
Mt 11:16	To what shall I compare this generation?
Mt 11:23	Will you be exalted to heaven?
Mt 12:3	Have you not read what David did when he and his companions were hungry, how he went into the house of God and ate the bread of offering which neither he nor his companions but only the priests could lawfully eat?
Mt 12:5	Or have you not read in the law that on the Sabbath the priests serving the temple violate the Sabbath and are innocent?
Mt 12:10	Is it lawful to cure on the Sabbath?
Mt 12:11	Which one of you who had a sheep that falls into a pit on the Sabbath will not take hold of it and lift it out?
Mt 12:26	If Satan drives out Satan, he is divided against himself; how then will his kingdom stand?

Mt 12:27	If I drive out demons by Beelzebul, by whom do your own people drive them out?
Mt 12:29	How can anyone enter a strong person's house and steal property unless that one first ties up the strong one?
Mt 12:34	You brood of vipers, how can you say good things when you are evil?
Mt 12:48	Who is my mother? Who are my brothers?
Mt 13:51	Do you understand all these things?
Mt 14:31	O you of little faith, why did you doubt?
Mt 15:3	Why do you break the commandment of God for the sake of your tradition?
Mt 15:16	Are even you still without understanding?
Mt 15:17	Do you not realize that everything that enters into the mouth passes into the stomach and is expelled into the latrine?
Mt 15:34	How many loaves do you have?
Mt 16:8	O you of little faith, why do you conclude among yourselves that it is because you have no bread?
Mt 16:9	Do you not understand? Do you not remember the five loaves for the five thousand and how many baskets you took up?
Mt 16:10	Or the seven loaves for the four thousand and how many baskets you took up?
Mt 16:11	How do you not comprehend that I was not speaking to you about bread?
Mt 16:13	Who do people say the Son of Man is?
Mt 16:15	But who do you say that I am?
Mt 16:26	What profit would there be for one to gain the whole world and forfeit his life?
Mt 16:26	What can one give in exchange for his life?

Mt 17:25   What is your opinion, Simon: From whom do the kings of the earth take tolls and census tax?

Mt 18:12   What is your opinion: If a person has a hundred sheep and one of them goes astray, will he not leave the ninety-nine in the hills and go in search of the stray?

Mt 20:14f   What if I wish to give this last one the same as you: am I not free to do as I wish with my own money?

Mt 20:15   Are you envious because I am generous?

Mt 20:20   What do you wish?

Mt 20:22   Can you drink the cup that I am going to drink?

Mt 20:32   What do you want me to do for you?

Mt 21:16   Have you never read the text: Out of the mouths of infants and nurslings you have brought forth praise?

Mt 21:25   Where was John's baptism from: was it of heavenly or of human origin?

Mt 21:28ff What is your opinion: which of the two did his father's will?

Mt 21:40   What will the owner of the vineyard do to those tenants when he comes?

Mt 21:42   Did you never read the Scriptures: The stone that builders rejected has become the cornerstone; by the Lord this has been done and it is wonderful in our eyes?

Mt 22:12   My friend, how is it that you came in here without a wedding garment?

Mt 22:18   Why are you testing me, you hypocrites?

Mt 22:20   Whose image is this and whose inscription?

Mt 22:31f   Concerning the resurrection did you not read what was said to you by God: I am the God of Abraham and the God of Isaac and the God of Jacob?

Mt 22:42   What do you think about the Messiah: whose son is he?

Mt 22:43ff   How then does David, in the Spirit, call him "Lord" . . . if David calls him "Lord," how is he his son?

Mt 23:17   Fools and blind ones, which is greater: the gold or the shrine sanctifying the gold?

Mt 23:33   You serpents, you brood of vipers, how can you escape from the judgment of Gehenna?

Mt 24:45   Who then is the faithful and prudent slave whom the lord put over his household to give them food in season?

Mt 25:27   Should you not have put my silver pieces in the bank so that coming I would receive mine with interest?

Mt 26:10   Why do you trouble the woman?

Mt 26:40   So you could not watch with me for one hour?

Mt 26:53   Do you think that I cannot ask my Father and he will now provide me with more than twelve legions of angels?

Mt 26:54   How then may the Scriptures be fulfilled which say that it must be in this way?

Mt 26:55   Have you come out as against a robber with swords and clubs to take me?

The Gospel of Saint Mark

Mk 2:8   Why are you thinking such things in your hearts?

Mk 2:9	Which is it easier to say to the paralytic: Your sins are forgiven you, or Rise, pick up your mat and walk?
Mk 2:19	Can the wedding guests fast while the bridegroom is with them?
Mk 2:25f	Have you never read what David did when he was in need and he and his companions were hungry; how he entered the house of God in the days of Abiathar, high priest and ate the loaves set before the Lord which it is not lawful to eat except if you are a priest, and he gave them to those with him?
Mk 3:4	Is it lawful on Sabbaths to do good or to do evil, to save life or to kill?
Mk 3:23	How can Satan expel Satan?
Mk 3:33	Who are my mother and brothers?
Mk 4:13	Do you not understand this parable? Then how will you understand any of the parables?
Mk 4:21	Is a lamp brought in to be placed under a bushel basket or under a bed and not to be placed on a lampstand?
Mk 4:30	To what shall we compare the kingdom of God or what parable can we use for it?
Mk 4:40	Why are you fearful like this; how have you not faith?
Mk 5:9	What is your name?
Mk 5:30	Who has touched my clothes?
Mk 6:38	How many loaves do you have?
Mk 7:18	Are you also undiscerning?
Mk 7:18f	Do you not understand that everything entering a person from the outside cannot defile him because it does not enter into the heart

but into the stomach and goes out into the latrine, purging all foods?

Mk 8:5   How many loaves do you have?

Mk 8:12   Why does this generation seek a sign?

Mk 8:17ff   Why do you conclude that it is because you have no loaves? Do you not yet understand and realize? Have your hearts been hardened? Do you have eyes and see not, have ears and hear not? And do you not remember when I broke the five loaves for the five thousand, how many full baskets of fragments did you take?

Mk 8:20   When I broke the seven for the four thousand, how many baskets full of fragments did you take?

Mk 8:21   Do you not yet realize?

Mk 8:23   Do you see anything?

Mk 8:27   Who do people say that I am?

Mk 8:29   But you, who do you say that I am?

Mk 8:36   What profits it a person to gain the whole world and forfeit his or her soul?

Mk 8:37   For what might a person give in exchange for his or her soul?

Mk 9:12   How has it been written concerning the Son of Man, that many things he should suffer and be set at naught?

Mk 9:16   What are you debating with them?

Mk 9:19   O unbelieving generation, how long shall I be with you, how long shall I endure you?

Mk 9:21   How long has this been happening to him?

Mk 9:33   What were you debating on the way?

Mk 9:49   If salt becomes insipid, with what will it be seasoned?

Mk 10:4   What did Moses command you?

Mk 10:36	What do you wish me to do for you?
Mk 10:38	Can you drink the cup that I drink or be baptized with the baptism with which I am baptized?
Mk 10:51	What do you want me to do for you?
Mk 11:17	Has it not been written: My house shall be called a house of prayer for all the nations?
Mk 11:30	Was John's baptism of heaven or of human origin?
Mk 12:9	What will the lord of the vineyard do?
Mk 12:10	Have you not read this scripture: A stone which the ones building rejected, this became the cornerstone, by the Lord has this been done and it is wonderful in our eyes?
Mk 12:15	Why do you tempt me?
Mk 12:16	Whose image and inscription is this?
Mk 12:24	Do you err not knowing the Scriptures nor the power of God?
Mk 12:26	But concerning the dead rising, did you not read in the Book of Moses how at the bush God said to him: I am the God of Abraham and the God of Isaac and the God of Jacob?
Mk 12:35	How do the scribes say that the Christ is the son of David?
Mk 12:37	David himself calls him Lord, how then is he his son?
Mk 13:2	Do you see these great buildings?
Mk 14:14	Where is my guestroom where I may eat the Passover with my disciples?
Mk 14:37	Simon, do you sleep? Could you not watch one hour?
Mk 14:48	As against a robber have you come with swords and clubs to arrest me?

Mk 15:34	*Eloi, eloi, lama sabachthani?* My God, my God, why do you forsake me?

The Gospel of Saint Luke

Lk 2:49	Why did you seek me? Did you not know I must be about my father's affairs?
Lk 5:22	Why do you question in your hearts?
Lk 5:23	What is easier: to say: Your sins have been forgiven you, or to say: Rise and walk?
Lk 6:2	Why do you do what is not lawful on the Sabboth?
Lk 6:3	Have you not read what David did when he and those with him were hungry?
Lk 6:9	I ask you if it is lawful on the Sabboth to do good or to do evil, to save life or to destroy?
Lk 6:32	If you love those loving you, what thanks is due to you there?
Lk 6:33	If you do good to those doing good to you, what thanks is due to you there?
Lk 6:34	If you lend to those from whom you hope to receive, what thanks is due to you there?
Lk 6:39	Can a blind person guide a blind one; will not both fall into a ditch?
Lk 6:41	Why do you see the mote in your brother's eye but do not heed the beam in your own eye?
Lk 6:42	How can you say to your brother: Let me take out the mote in your eye, not seeing the beam in your own eye?
Lk 6:46	Why do you call me: Lord, Lord, and do not what I say?
Lk 7:24	What did you go into the desert to see—a reed being shaken in the wind?

Lk 7:25	What did you go out to see—a man clothed in soft garments?
Lk 7:26	What did you go out to see—a prophet?
Lk 7:31	To what then may I liken the men of this generation and to what are they like?
Lk 7:42	Which of them [two forgiven debts] will love him more?
Lk 7:44	Do you see this woman?
Lk 8:25	Where is your faith?
Lk 8:30	What is your name?
Lk 8:45	Who is the one touching me?
Lk 9:18	Whom do the crowds say that I am?
Lk 9:20	But you, whom do you say that I am?
Lk 9:25	What is the profit to a person who gains the whole world but loses or suffers the loss of himself?
Lk 9:41	O generation unbelieving and perverted, how long shall I be with you and endure you?
Lk 10:15	And you, Capernaum, were you not lifted to heaven?
Lk 10:26	In the Law, what has been written? How do you read it?
Lk 10:36	Who of these three does it seem to you became neighbor to the one who falls among the robbers?
Lk 11:5	Who of you has a friend who comes to him at midnight and says to him: Friend, lend me three loaves since a friend of mine has come to me off a journey and I have nothing to set before him; and the one within answering might say: Do not cause me trouble; the door has now been shut and my children are with me in bed; I cannot get up to give to you?

Lk 11:11	Which father among you when your son asks for a fish, will hand him not a fish but a serpent? Or he asks for an egg, will hand him a scorpion?
Lk 11:18	And if Satan is divided against himself, how will his kingdom stand?
Lk 11:19	But if I expel the demons by Beelzebub, by what do your sons expel?
Lk 12:6	Are not five sparrows sold for two farthings?
Lk 12:14	Man, who appointed me a judge or a divider over you?
Lk 12:25	And which of you being anxious can add a cubit to your stature?
Lk 12:26	If therefore you can not do the least thing, why are you anxious concerning other things?
Lk 12:42	Who then is the faithful steward, the prudent one, whom the lord will appoint over his household attendants to give out the portion of food in due time?
Lk 12:51	Do you think that I have come to give peace on the earth?
Lk 12:56	Hypocrites, you know how to discern the face of the earth and of the heavens, how is it that you do not know how to discern this time?
Lk 12:57	And why, even among yourselves, you do not judge what is righteous?
Lk 13:2	Do you think that these Galilaeans were sinners above all the Galilaeans because they suffered these things?
Lk 13:4	Or those eighteen on whom the tower of Siloam fell, killing them, do you think they were debtors above all the other men dwelling in Jerusalem?

Lk 13:7   Why does it even spoil the ground?

Lk 13:15   Hypocrites, does not each one of you on the Sabbath loosen his ox or ass from the manger and lead it away to drink?

Lk 13:16   And this woman, a daughter of Abraham, who Satan held bound eighteen years, was it not fitting that she be loosed from this bond on the Sabbath day?

Lk 13:18   What is the Kingdom of God like, to what may I liken it?

Lk 13:20   To what may I liken the Kingdom of God?

Lk 14:3   Is it lawful to heal on the Sabbath or not?

Lk 14:5   Which of you, whose son or ox falls into a pit, will not pull him up on the Sabbath day?

Lk 14:28   For who of you, wishing to build a tower does not, sitting down, first reckon the cost, if he or she has enough for completion?

Lk 14:31   Or what king going to attack another king in war does not, sitting down, explore if he is able with ten thousand to meet the one coming upon him with twenty thousand?

Lk 15:4   What man among you, having a hundred sheep and losing one of them, does not leave the ninety-nine in the desert and go after the one who has been lost until he finds it?

Lk 15:8   Or what woman, having ten drachmas, if she loses one drachma, does not light a lamp and sweep the house and seek carefully until she finds it?

Lk 16:2   What is this I hear about you?

Lk 16:11   If you have not been faithful in regard to the mammon of unrighteousness who will entrust the true to you?

Lk 16:12	And if in regard to what belongs to another you have been unfaithful, who will give you yours?
Lk 17:7	But which one of you having a slave ploughing or herding, when he comes in off the farm will say to him: Come up and sit down; rather will you not say to him: prepare something that I may dine and gird yourself to serve me until I have eaten and drunk and after this you eat and drink?
Lk 17:9	Does he have thanks for the slave because the slave did the things commanded?
Lk 17:17	Were not ten cleansed, but where are the nine?
Lk 17:18	Was not only this stranger found returning to give glory to God?
Lk 18:7	Will not God vindicate God's holy ones who cry to God day and night and be patient with them?
Lk 18:8	Nevertheless, when the Son of Man comes will he find the faith on the earth?
Lk 18:19	Why do you call me good?
Lk 18:41	What do you wish me to do for you?
Lk 19:22	You knew that I am an exacting man, taking what I did not lay down and reaping what I did not sew?
Lk 19:23	And why did you not place my money on a [banker's] table?
Lk 20:4	The baptism of John, was it from heaven or was it of human origin?
Lk 20:15	What therefore will the owner of the vineyard do to them?
Lk 20:17	What then has been written: The stone which the ones building rejected, this came to be the cornerstone?

Lk 20:24	Show me a denarius: of whom has it an image and superscription?
Lk 20:41	How do they say that the Christ is David's son?
Lk 22:27	For who is greater: the one reclining or the one serving? Is it not the one reclining?
Lk 22:35	When I sent you without a purse and a wallet and sandals, were you short of anything?
Lk 22:46	Why do you sleep?
Lk 22:48	Judas, do you betray the Son of Man with a kiss?
Lk 22:52	Do you come out as against a robber with swords and clubs?
Lk 23:31	If they do these things when the tree is full of sap, what may happen in the dry time?
Lk 24:17	What are these words which you exchange with each other as you walk?
Lk 24:19	What things?
Lk 24:26	Behoved it not the Christ to suffer these things and to enter into his glory?
Lk 24:38	Why have you been troubled and why do thoughts arise in your heart?
Lk 24:41	Have you any food here?

The Gospel of Saint John

Jn 1:38	What do you seek?
Jn 1:50	Because I told you I saw you underneath the fig tree, do you believe?
Jn 2:4	What is that to me and to you, Woman?
Jn 3:10	You are a teacher of Israel and you do not know these things?
Jn 3:12	If I told you earthly things and you do not believe, how if I tell you heavenly things will you believe?

Jn 5:6	Do you wish to become whole?
Jn 5:44	How can you believe who receive glory from one another and do not seek the glory from the one God?
Jn 5:47	But if the writings of that one [Moses] you do not believe, how will you believe my words?
Jn 6:5	Where may we buy loaves so that these may eat?
Jn 6:61	Does this offend you?
Jn 6:62	What then if you see the Son of Man ascending where he was at first?
Jn 6:67	Do you not also wish to go?
Jn 6:69	Did not I choose you the Twelve?
Jn 7:19	Did not Moses give you the Law? Why do you seek to kill me?
Jn 7:23	If a man receives circumcision on a Sabbath the law of Moses is not broken, why are you angry with me because I made a whole man healthy on the Sabbath?
Jn 8:10	Woman, where are they, has no one condemned you?
Jn 8:43	Why do you not comprehend my speech?
Jn 8:46	Who of you reproves me because of sin? If I speak truth why do you not believe me?
Jn 9:35	Do you believe in the Son of Man?
Jn 10:32	Many of the Father's good works I showed you, for which one of them do you stone me?
Jn 10:34	Is it not written in your law: I said, you are gods?
Jn 10:35	If he called gods those with whom the word of God was, and the scripture cannot be broken, do you say to him whom the Father sanctified

and sent into the world, You blaspheme, because I said, I am the Son of God?

Jn 11:9   Are there not twelve hours in the day?

Jn 11:25f I am the resurrection and the life; the one believing in me even if that one should die will live and everyone living and believing in me does not die unto the age; do you believe this?

Jn 11:34   Where have you put him?

Jn 11:40   Did I not tell you, if you believe you will see the glory of God?

Jn 12:27   And now my soul has been troubled and what may I say: Father save me from this hour?

Jn 13:12   Do you know what I have done to you?

Jn 13:38   Will you lay down your life for me?

Jn 14:9   I am so long with you and you do not know me, Philip?

Jn 14:10   Do you not believe that I am in the Father and the Father is in me?

Jn 18:11   The cup which the Father has given me, shall I not drink it?

Jn 18:21   Why do you question me?

Jn 18:34   Of yourself do you say this or have others told you about me?

Jn 20:15   Woman, why are you weeping? Whom do you seek?

Jn 21:5   Children, have you no fish?

Jn 21:15   Simon of John, do you love me more than these?

Jn 21:16   Simon of John, do you love me?

Jn 21:17   Simon of John, do you love me?

Jn 21:22   If I wish him to remain until I come, what is that to you?

The Method of Lectio Divina

It is well to keep the Sacred Scriptures enthroned in our home in a place of honor as a Real Presence of the Word in our midst.

1. Take the Sacred Text with reverence and call upon Holy Spirit.
2. For ten minutes (or longer, if you are so drawn) listen to the Lord speaking to you through the Text, and respond to him.
3. At the end of the time, choose a word or phrase (perhaps one will have been "given" to you) to take with you, and thank the Lord for being with you and speaking to you.

More briefly we might put it this way:

1. Come into the Presence and call upon Holy Spirit.
2. Listen for ten minutes.
3. Thank the Lord and take a "word."

Centering Prayer

FINDING PEACE AT THE CENTER

At that Last Supper, Jesus told his disciples—all of us: "I no longer call you servants, but friends, because I make known to you all that the Father has made known to me"—all the secrets of my heart. We have been made for a deep intimate friendship with the Lord. Our hearts long for it. We are not content with just listening to the Lord's words, no matter how wonderful they are. We want a deeper, more experiential union with God. It is like any true friendship, as it grows it needs to go beyond words and doing things together and for each other. The image Scripture has frequently used is that of the marital embrace, that total being to each other. We need those times of prayer when we listen not just with our ears, our eyes, our minds, but more with our hearts, with our whole being.

This is contemplative prayer or prayer of the heart. It is a prayer of being. The tradition has passed down to us a simple way of entering into this kind of prayer. This traditional way is called today, Centering Prayer.

Centering Prayer is a very simple way of prayer which can be used by anyone who wants to be with God, to experience God's love and presence. It is a prayer of longing that leads into Presence.

First of all, we settle ourselves down quietly. Most of us pray best sitting down, but take any posture that works well for you. It is best if the back is fairly straight and well supported. If we gently close our eyes, we immediately begin to quiet down, for we use a lot of our psychic energy in seeing.

Once we are settled, we turn our attention to the Lord present within us. We know God is there by faith, that is, we know God is there because Jesus said so. In love we turn ourselves over to the Lord. For these twenty minutes we are all God's. God can do with us whatever God wants. This prayer is a pure gift, a gift of self in love.

In order to be able to abide quietly and attentively with our Beloved, we use a love word, a prayer word—a simple word that expresses our being to the Lord in love. It might well be our favorite name: Lord, Jesus, Father, Love . . . whatever is meaningful for us. We just let that word be there, to keep us attentive to the Lord. It is not an effortful proclamation or a constantly repeated *mantra,* but rather a sigh of love, a murmur of love, a "being to," a directive from the mind to the heart to be all there with the Lord.

Whenever during the time of our prayer we become aware of anything else, we simply use our love word to return to the Lord. Some days we will have to use the word constantly, there may be a lot of commotion around us or in us. No matter. Each time we use it, each time we return to God, it is perfect gift of self to God in love. Other days we may not need to use our word much at all. Fine! It really makes no difference. Simply, these twenty minutes are all God's to do with us as God likes. We do not seek anything for ourselves. It is pure gift. It is not in the twenty minutes we will be aware of things. All our attention is on God. It is outside the time of prayer that we will begin to see the difference, as the fruits of the Spirit begin to flourish in our lives.

At the end of our twenty minutes, we do not want to jump right back into activity. We have gone very deep, even if we do not seem to sense it. So we want to end our prayer very gently. I suggest praying interiorly, very slowly, the *Our Father*. Let each phrase come forth with all its meaning. In this the Lord will teach us much. And the deep peace of our contemplative prayer will flow into our active lives.

To sum up:

CENTERING PRAYER

Sit relaxed and quiet.

1. Be in faith and love to God who dwells in the center of our being.
2. Take up a love word and let it be gently present, supporting our being to God in faith-filled love.
3. Whenever we become aware of anything, simply, gently return to the Lord with the use of our prayer word.

At the end of twenty minutes let the *Our Father* pray itself within us.

This is a prayer of experience, so we can only know it by experience. We always urge people learning this prayer to take a stand that they will practice the prayer faithfully, twice a day, for a month or two, to give God a chance to show them what God wants to do in their lives through the prayer. Then at the end of the time let them look—perhaps with a close friend or spiritual guide, for someone else can usually see better than we—and see what has been the fruit of the prayer in their lives. If the way they were praying before was producing better fruit, they are not hesitant to return to it. But if this simple prayer of attentive love has been good for them, then by all means they are to continue it. The important thing is that we do pray regularly and allow God to be to us the source of love, life, peace and happiness that God wants to be and that we so much want.

May you find great peace and joy at the Center. Let us hold each other in caring prayer.

Some Helpful Reading

Bernard of Clairvaux, *The Works of Bernard of Clairvaux,* tr. Michael Casey et. al. Spencer MA–Kalamazoo MI: Cistercian Publications, 1969—.

Casey, Michael, *Sacred Reading. The Ancient Art of Lectio Divina.* Melbourne: HarperCollins, 1995.

Illich, Ivan, *In the Vineyard of the Text. A Commentary to Hugh's Didascalion.* Chicago: The University of Chicago Press, 1993.

Keating, Thomas, *Awakenings.* San Francisco: Harpercollins, 1990.

    The Kingdom of God is Like. New York: Crossroad, 1993.

    Reawakenings. New York: Crossroads, 1992.

Merton, Thomas, *Opening the Bible.* Collegeville, MI: The Liturgical Press, 1970.

Pennington, M. Basil, *A Place Apart. Monastic Prayer and Practice for Everyone.* Liguori, MO: Ligouri, 1998.

    Awake in the Spirit. A Personal Handbook on Prayer. New York: Crossroad, 1996.

    Breaking Bread. The Table Talk of Jesus. San Francisco: Harper and Row, 1986.

    Call to the Center. New York: Doubleday, 1990; Hyde Park, NY: New City Press, 1995.

    Centering Prayer. Renewing An Ancient Christian Prayer Form. New York: Doubleday, 1980.

    Lectio Divina. Renewing the Ancient Practice of Praying the Scriptures. New York: Crossroad, 1998.

    The Manual of Life. The New Testament for Daily Living. New York: Paulist Press, 1985.

Reininger, Gustave, *Centering Prayer in Daily Life and Ministry.* New York: Continuum, 1998.

William of Saint Thierry, *The Works of William of Saint Thierry,* tr. Penelope Lawson et al. Spencer MA–Kalamazoo MI: Cistercian Publications, 1969—.